CREATIVE BIBLE LESSONS IN EZEKIEL

ANCIENT REVELATIONS FOR A POSTMODERN GENERATION

ANNA AVEN HOWARD

youth specialties

Creative Bible Lessons in Ezekiel: Ancient Revelations for a Postmodern Generation
Copyright © 2007 by Youth Specialties

Youth Specialties products, 300 S. Pierce St., El Cajon, CA 92020 are published by Zondervan, 5300 Patterson Ave.
SE, Grand Rapids, MI 49530.

ISBN-10: 0-310-26960-1
ISBN-13: 978-0-310-26960-1

Creative Team: Erika Hueneke, Rich Cairnes, Dave Urbanski, Anna Hammond, and David Conn
Cover Design by Holly Sharp/SharpSeven Design

Printed in the United States of America

07 08 09 10 11 12 • 23 22 21 20 19 18 17 16 15 14 13 12 11 10 9 8 7 6 5 4 3 2 1

Chris & Hannah
Kidd

CREATIVE BIBLE LESSONS
IN EZEKIEL

ANCIENT REVELATIONS FOR A
POSTMODERN GENERATION

PERFECT FOR SUNDAY SCHOOL, YOUTH MEETINGS, SMALL GROUPS, AND MORE!

ANNA AVEN HOWARD

ZONDERVAN®

ZONDERVAN.com/
AUTHORTRACKER
follow your favorite authors

youth
specialties
.com

DEDICATION

To my parents, who never stopped believing I would write a book.

To my brother, Josh, for unending support.

And to my husband, Jody, for the countless hours of bouncing ideas around and discussing illustrations with me as I wrote.

SPECIAL THANKS

And thanks to Chap for giving me the idea to write this particular book.

"I will put my Spirit in you and you will live…"
Ezekiel 37:14

"And the name of the city from that time on will be:
THE LORD IS THERE."
Ezekiel 48:35

CONTENTS

JOURNALING EXERCISE HANDOUTS

HOW TO USE THIS BOOK
(AND WHAT YOU NEED TO KNOW BEFORE YOU START)

WHY EZEKIEL?

As a book that begins with a description akin to a UFO sighting and ends with a river that can flow over mountains, Ezekiel is an oft-neglected book when it comes to teaching material. While some portions of the book are difficult to explain, the pictures this prophet's actions paint provide vivid illustrations of who God is, who we are, and our responsibility in relation to understanding who God is.

In Ezekiel, in fact, we find a continual interplay between this notion of who God is and what that means in terms of our lives and relationships with him. If we replace the rebellious nation of Israel in these prophetic images with ourselves, we find a message with the potential to strike us to our very cores. While we may not have literal idols set up in literal temples, our bodies are supposed to be temples of the Holy Spirit. What kind of idols then are we setting up in our hearts? What does it take to drive God away? How would our views of God change, knowing that even after we've driven him away and our lives are suffering as a result, God follows us into that place of exile and pleads with us to come back because he loves us so much? What is a covenant, and why is it essential to understand that God has made a covenant with us? What does God ask of us for our nation? What does God ask of our peers?

Is it a stretch to apply spiritual metaphors to the reality of the temple worship and traditions of the Old Testament? I believe this is perfectly acceptable based on Hebrews 9. Everything in the Old Testament is a pattern of that which was to come. Many riches can be gleaned from this image-heavy book, and the illustrations God has Ezekiel perform lend themselves particularly well to application as metaphors for our lives as the people of God and as temples of the Holy Spirit.

SOME THINGS TO CONSIDER

Sometime when I reached the middle of Ezekiel, I was struck by the "otherness" of God. This Bible book gives a vivid depiction of a God who won't fit neatly into the little categories we have in mind for him. God won't stay in a box; and a lot of times in Ezekiel, God most definitely doesn't look like our buddy. God acts for the sake of his own name, destroys his own city and temple, and then brings the people back, not because they repent, but because God wants to vindicate himself. What are we supposed to do with this unruly view of God? In Ezekiel, is God less loving and more motivated by the need to adjust the Israelite nation's view of the divine? Can we reconcile this to the New Testament, which tells us that God is love (1 John 4:8)?

I believe the answer not only is "yes, we can," but also "yes, we *must*." If Jesus Christ is the same yesterday, today, and forever (Hebrews 13:8) and Jesus is the Word made flesh who was with God in the beginning (John 1:1-2, 14), then not only is the New Testament idea of Jesus an accurate view of God…the more enigmatic one that we find in parts of the Old Testament is as well. Actually, this enigma is everywhere in the Bible; it's often easier to look only at the Gospels, concentrate on the life of Jesus, and believe there's less to resolve. Of course, we still have to explain the whole "100 percent God" plus "100 percent man" equaling "100 percent Jesus" thing, but, hey, since when was that difficult? (Umm, let me rephrase that…)

So, is this view of God in Ezekiel a far cry from the "buddy Jesus" of our Sunday-school-flannelgraph days? Well, yes. And no. I believe that if we do have a "buddy Jesus" sort of outlook, we need to get over it. Yes, Jesus wants to be in an intimate relationship with each and every one of us, but we have to continually understand that this carpenter from Galilee who wants to know us and have us know him is the creator of the universe and continues to sustain it—and all of us.

Far from something that makes our relationships with God more difficult for us, the otherness of God—understanding the awesome splendor and majesty of God—should excite us when we think about the fact that this same majestic God loves us so passionately that he died for us. The same God who spoke the universe into existence wants to speak into our hearts. The one who created the breathtaking sunsets, dreamed up the oceans, and formed the mountain peaks knit us together in our mothers' wombs, taking personal care to form us and create a unique plan for each of our lives (Psalm 139:13, 16).

And this outlook is the view Ezekiel gives us, despite some difficult passages and strange, disturbing imagery. What we see in this book is this awesome God—who is totally other and yet is passionately in love with you and with me.

FORMAT OF *CBL IN EZEKIEL*

Each session is formatted with the following headings: Overview, Set Up, Background for Leaders, and Making It Live for Your Students. Under the Background for Leaders and the Making It Live for Your Students headings, you'll find a series of subheadings that are unique points for each session.

If you're familiar with the other books in the Creative Bible Lessons series, then you'll notice the format of the sessions in this book is a little different. Because Ezekiel is an unfamiliar book for a lot of people, it seemed more background information was needed, so I divided each session into two parts.

The first is a fairly extensive background, provided for session leaders, which contains research from several commentaries and other books discussing the theology of the prophets (see Bibliography). More information is included in these background sections than you can probably use with your average youth group or Sunday school time, but this way you'll be armed with more information in case of questions. It will also allow you to tailor the sessions to the interests and needs of your group.

The second part contains some combination of teaching, illustrations, activities, movie clips, and song suggestions. Each section also contains a journaling exercise with a handout of questions for your students to consider.

USING ADDITIONAL TEXTS

Under the Additional Texts heading, you'll find a New Testament verse or passage that goes along with the session's subject, which is essential to discuss at some point in your talk, depending on how you choose to structure it (see Using Background for Leaders). Any additional texts are mentioned in either the Background for Leaders section or the Making It Live for Your Students section.

NOTE: As you go through each section, you may at times notice references to even more texts than are listed. I included these Scriptures merely for your benefit, so you can see what part of the Bible I'm referring to or paraphrasing. Some of these texts tie in ideas from the New Testament, while some point to background information. So if you want to check them out, you have the references.

UNDERSTANDING THE OVERVIEW

This notes the "big picture" of where each session is going. It'll be helpful to keep that in mind as you prepare your session, because it helps keep you focused.

USING THE SET UP

This section notes all the materials, movie clips, songs, music videos, etc., that you'll need for the session. Be sure to check this well in advance of your meeting time, since some are more complicated than others.

USING BACKGROUND FOR LEADERS AND MAKING IT LIVE FOR YOUR STUDENTS

Before reading over the session structure, read the portion of Ezekiel listed under the chapter heading. Then read the Background for Leaders section, making an outline of the points you want to use in your talk. With that rough outline in hand, read the next section: Making It Live for Your Students. It's kind of a rough outline itself, but it's even more effective if you use it as a sort of pointer, fitting the illustrations into your own outline from the Background for Leaders section. The selections in bold are suggestions for actual scripts you can use with your group to flesh out your talk.

GETTING THE MOST OUT OF THE JOURNALING EXERCISES

To close each of the sessions is a journaling exercise with a handout of questions. Your students can use a copy of the handout to write on, they can bring their own journals, or you could create journals of your own by putting together an Ezekiel booklet with the questions in it and blank pages. Putting a booklet together would take some advance prep work of one to two weeks before starting this series. Alternatively, if you have or could design stickers for your youth group, purchase inexpensive spiral notebooks (you can cheaply buy six packs of one-subject notebooks at any office store), put the stickers on the front, and then hand out the journaling sheets for each session for the kids to work with but not write on.

Obviously, it's easier to copy the sheets and hand them out, but journaling is an important discipline and practice. If you can get your kids to journal in a book rather than on a loose sheet of paper, they're more likely to keep it and then look back at what they've learned and the things they've said to God over the weeks they traveled through Ezekiel. (And, who knows, maybe they'll decide to start journaling for themselves even after this series is done.)

OVERVIEW

If we get a grasp on who God is, it will greatly affect how we live. Ezekiel saw an overwhelming vision of God, received a commission as a prophet, and went on to spread God's word among his people. We are called just as Ezekiel was to understand who God is and spread the message to our people.

SET UP

ACTIVITY

• Blank paper and markers or colored pencils for each student

• Bibles (or a copy of Ezekiel 1 printed out for each student who may not have direct access to a Bible during the session)

MOVIE

• *Bruce Almighty* (NOTE: I recommend clips from this film in three different sessions. If you think you'll use these clips, I highly recommend buying the film. Plus, you could use it for an optional movie-and-discussion night at some point during the series.)

• "Facedown" by Matt Redman (*Facedown*, 2004)

SECTION 1: BACKGROUND FOR LEADERS

God appeared to Ezekiel when Ezekiel was in exile with his people in Babylon. That means God himself was in exile. God was, in effect, homeless in that he had allowed the people so much freedom that they had kicked him out of their hearts and out of the temple, thus severing the relationship from their side. And what does God do? He follows them. They reject God, and God follows them into exile. As we go through the book of Ezekiel, God goes to great lengths to get the attention of those he loves to keep them from continuing in their self-destructive behavior.

The fact that God followed them into exile doesn't mean there are no consequences to walking out of a relationship with God. But God allows those consequences. For the Israelites, the consequence was exile. However, here's the amazing-grace part: God had every right to stand in the promised land waving good-bye as the Israelites were marched off into exile, and then like the wounded lover, sit there with his arms crossed and wait for the Israelites to try to fight their way out of the mess they'd gotten themselves into and come crawling back to him (Ezekiel 6:9). God could have, but he didn't.

Ezekiel's adventure takes place in the land of the Babylonians, far from his native home. He and his people had been carried off into exile because of their disobedience to God. When the people stopped following God, God lifted his hand of protection, and the Israelites' enemies conquered them. In this case, the Babylonians had taken some of the people off into exile and left some of them in Israel after conquering them. This was a tactic to demoralize the people and spread them so far apart that they would be unlikely to attempt a revolt.

So that's the background for why we find this young man Ezekiel standing alone by the Chebar River one balmy day, July 31, 593 BC,[1] somewhere in his 30th year (1:1), when God shows up. We can only imagine what that must have been like. We have to wonder what Ezekiel was thinking. He was carried off into captivity because of the actions of his fellow citizens of Israel, and now, just at the time when he should have been taking over responsibilities as a priest at the temple of God, here he is, by himself, hanging out by the river.

[1] See footnote on 1:1 in the New Living Translation.

You see, Ezekiel was a Levite, the son of a priest (verse 3), and thus destined to be a priest himself. Young men were initiated into the priesthood at the age of 30, but here in a foreign land with no temple, there's no way for Ezekiel to carry out his calling and role in the community.

Or was there? Ezekiel and his fellow captives were already entering their fifth year of captivity (verse 2). God could have come for his chat with Ezekiel before now. And yet, he shows up in Ezekiel's 30th year. Coincidence? Could it be coincidence that God shows up to give Ezekiel his calling at the time when Ezekiel should have been initiated into the priesthood? Consider this: Even when you're in captivity, whether as a consequence of your own actions or a result of other people's choices, God hasn't forgotten his plan for you or what he has called you to do—and God can show up, right there in the middle of your captivity, and go right on fulfilling his promise for your life.

And not only is God showing up to initiate Ezekiel into his calling exactly when he was supposed to be initiated, but God also appeared to Ezekiel in captivity! This is a God who doesn't sit in a temple and pout because his people have disobeyed him and gotten themselves carried off into captivity; this is a God who comes to his people, comes to us—even in the midst of the consequences of our own actions—all because he wants to call us back to himself.

GOD IS OTHER AND YET DESIRES A RELATIONSHIP WITH US

In Ezekiel 1, God is above the platform, above these strange creatures, and is the source of all the strange light and sounds that Ezekiel sees and hears. And yet, God appears in the form or shape of a human (verse 26), which Ezekiel can glimpse beyond all of this "otherness." This is a beautiful picture of the majesty and splendor of our God, combined with his continual desire to draw broken and sinful humans back to himself. We're used to thinking of this in terms of Jesus dying on the cross for us, and of course, that's *the* event that enables us to be reconciled to God; but this chapter in Ezekiel, while probably the most dramatic, is just one of many instances throughout the Bible where God goes to great lengths to communicate to his people. Not only do we see God here in a form that Ezekiel can recognize, but after this vision God comes close enough that Ezekiel is completely overwhelmed, falls on his face in worship, and hears a voice speaking—God speaking—directly to him. And this God is still speaking to you and to me as we study his Word, begin to recognize his heartbeat, and learn to tune our ears to his whisperings so that we, too, with Ezekiel, can glimpse a majesty and glory beyond anything we could have imagined—a glory and a majesty that will sweep us off our feet as we realize this is our God, and he is madly in love with us.

SECTION 2: MAKING IT LIVE FOR YOUR STUDENTS

INTRODUCTION

Put blank paper and copies of Ezekiel chapter 1 on each seat. Place containers of colored markers or colored pencils where your students have easy access to them.

Say: *Close your eyes. Picture in your head all the things you're hearing.* Then read all of Ezekiel 1 out loud to them. *Draw your interpretation of what you just heard.* Have them hang on to their pictures for a minute until the group gets more into the guts of the chapter.

DIGGING IN: HOW BIG IS YOUR GOD?

• Ask: *What kinds of questions have you had about God?* Make sure you fill in some of your own questions about God when the students have finished.

• *Is it safe to say that some things about God are hard to understand? What kinds of things?* If students don't bring these things up, you might want to add things that would make entire sessions in themselves, such as how God can exist in three persons and still be one God. Or try adding 100 percent God and 100 percent man to equal 100 percent Jesus.

• Say: *Could it actually be comforting that we can't understand God?*

• *I mean, how many of us can completely understand ourselves?*

• *Have you ever been upset about something and weren't sure why?* (Caution: Don't let them tell stories; this is just to get them thinking about the fact that they don't understand themselves.)

• *If we can't even understand ourselves, would we want to worship a God who we could understand?*

• *Would that kind of God be even smaller than we are?*

• *There are mysteries about God, certainly, but it's these mysteries that play a big part in making us want to worship God. In fact, Ezekiel's vision made him fall flat on his face in response to such awesome glory and majesty.*

• Ask: *What can your God do?* If they don't answer right away, say something like: *We're talking about God, our God, and yet I think we place limits on God because we don't leave room for him to do things in our lives. Can God speak to us?* (Yes!) *Heal?* (Yes!) *Perform miracles?* (Yes!) *Raise someone from the dead?* (Yes!) *But how often we experience those things may depend on us.*

NOTE: It's important here not to fall into the trap of making it sound as though God acting in someone's life is entirely up to the person or how much faith that person has. The fact of the matter is, we can't understand God, and thus sometimes we may believe fully and be fully open to God doing something—say, healing a disease—and yet God doesn't, and the person dies. That's hard to reconcile when that person has suffered through so much and God doesn't seem to be responding. It's easy to blame the person and his supposed lack of faith when God doesn't respond as we think he should. The truth is, however, that God doesn't heal one person because she has more faith than the next person, and God doesn't refuse to heal another because he lacks faith. The bottom line is, we can't understand everything God does, but we can trust him.

THE KIND OF GOD WE HAVE

Explain: *If you look at the deities of the surrounding nations and compare them with Ezekiel's vision, there are some striking reasons why Ezekiel saw what he saw. For starters, at that time in the surrounding nations, the people held a very strong concept of a land/people/deity triangle. In their view, if the deity's power was to remain intact, this triangle had to be inseparable. Therein lies another view of why nations carried the people they conquered into exile: They were breaking the land/people/deity connection. The land belonged to the deity, and the people worshiped the local god or goddess in order to have good crops, blessings on their lives, and so forth. Out of the land, the deity had no power over the people, so if you can remove a people from their land, you can take them away from their god.*

But not this God. Not Yahweh, the God of Abraham, Isaac, and Jacob. Whether his people realized it or not—and most of them probably didn't—this God was not tied to the land. This point is brought home when he appears to Ezekiel in this chapter.

• *What are some of the things that stood out to you when you heard this chapter and as we drew what we heard? Let's look at what you guys drew…*Have your students explain their drawings. If your group is large, you can have them turn to people around them and explain, and then you can highlight the main things that got repeated, or you could call for some volunteers who would represent a good cross section of your group.

• *What do you suppose is the significance of the wheels?* Wheels = Motion

• *Notice the wheels don't turn, and yet the platform above them moves wherever God wants it to. What does this tell us about God?* God is free to come from wherever he likes and go wherever he likes. The four wheels speak of the four winds or the four points of the compass, demonstrating that God can go wherever he wants.

• *List some observations about the four living creatures.* Each of the four living creatures has four faces.

As the students list the faces, ask: *What's significant about these faces?* If they get stuck, explain each face as a student brings it up.

Human face: Human beings are the only ones created in God's image, with the ability to create and reason. This is the face that faces outward.

Lion face: Say: *List some of the things we know about lions.* Make sure you also highlight these things if they don't get said: The lion is a fierce beast that was a symbol of strength and courage. It was also considered sort of the king of wild beasts. The lion is the face on the right.

Ox face: Say: *What do you know about oxen?* If there's a "king" among cattle, then it's the ox, and the ox was a valuable domestic animal that frequently served as a symbol of both fertility and divinity in the surrounding cultures. The ox is the face on the left.

Eagle face: Say: *Tell me some characteristics of eagles.* The face on the back, then, is an eagle, and the eagle is a swift bird, likewise considered sort of a king of birds.

• *What is the main adjective used to describe these creatures?* It's important to note that these are the four *living* creatures.

• *What does this tell us about God?* This God is a God of life.

• Explain: *With these four supernatural beings that display the majesty of God, not one of them is an inanimate representation, nor are they meant to be worshiped—a far cry from the stone and wood images that represented the deities of the surrounding countries.*

• Summarize: *So in this vision, God has clearly shown himself to be not only entirely mobile, entirely different from people, and completely removed from the other deities of the surrounding nations, but also completely over the created order in that the living creatures are a unique hybrid of all creation because they represent both humans and the different orders of animals.*

Say: *Look at your drawings one more time.*

• Ask: *Is there anything you see in this passage that's different from how you're used to viewing God? Is there anything that surprises you?* The idea to draw out is that Ezekiel presents us with a picture of God that's not exactly the grandparent upstairs we sometimes imagine.

• If the students get stuck, you could say something like: *This God isn't strictly the "buddy" God whom we often make him out to be. But while he's entirely "other" and full of awesome majesty and glory, that doesn't make him the mean, judgmental God who's out to punish sinners whom we sometimes characterize him as. No, this completely powerful, divine God is so in love with his people that he has followed them into exile.*

WHERE DOES YOUR GOD LIVE?

Now explain exile by saying something like: *The people of Israel had turned away from God, and by doing that, they took themselves out from under his hand of protection. And so they ended up getting conquered by the Babylonians and carried off to a place that was far away from their home. Ezekiel is among these exiles when God shows up.*

• *Where do we usually picture God living?* A few students will likely say God lives in heaven.

• *Where is God in this passage?* In the middle of his people. If they get stuck, say: *Here in Ezekiel it's very clear that God wants to be among his people. This is a living, active, and present God who is with the people not only in a time of hardship—which exile certainly was—but in a time of hardship that they themselves had caused!*

• *We have some sort of concept that God is watching, but what difference does it make to know that he's not just watching, but he's right here?*

Then say: *The Israelites were in Babylon because of their sin against God. They had turned their backs on him and were worshiping other gods. Just as bad as infidelity in a marriage, idol worship was the Israelites effectively cheating on God. So God lifted his hand of protection and allowed the Israelites to be carried off into exile. The exile was a direct consequence of the peoples' choices to worship other gods.*

But God is there with his people even when they're in exile…

• *Now, someone tell me in your own words, what is exile?* Get a student or two to summarize back all the big concepts you just explained to them.

• *So, if exile is the result of the people's sin and God shows up in the middle of exile, what does this tell us about God?* This means God is with us even in the consequences of our actions.

• *Why would God want to be with us even in the consequences of what we've done?* Because he loves us and wants to call us back to him.

• Explain: *The consequences of the Israelites' actions don't disappear, and yet God is right there in the middle of them. This is a God who is so radically in love with his people that he will go into exile to try to reestablish the broken relationship that got them there in the first place. A God in exile…where else do you find that?*

MOVIE CLIP: *BRUCE ALMIGHTY*—HOW FAR DO YOU HAVE TO GO TO OUTRUN GOD?

Ask your students who have seen the movie to explain why Bruce got fired. Make sure to summarize their answers by saying: *Bruce was discontented with his job and with his life, and when he didn't get what he wanted, he vented on live television and got himself fired.*

• Ask: *Was Bruce responsible for what happened to him?*

Set up the clip by saying: *At this point in the film, Bruce has accused God of picking on him and ruining his life, saying God is like the mean kid with a magnifying glass frying the legs off of ants. Here's what happens next.*

Play the clip. START [00:21:06] END [00:24:59] (Pager scene)

• Say: *Bruce had asked God some questions…asked him for help and guidance… screamed at him to answer…and then Bruce's pager goes off. Is this an answer? How do you think Bruce was expecting God to answer?* Make sure you summarize answers by pointing out that Bruce was looking for a miracle. He wanted something with lots of bang and snap, and what he got was a page from an unknown number.

• *Do we ever ask God a question and forget to look for the answer?*

• *What annoys Bruce about the pager?* It keeps beeping and beeping.

• Explain: *God is patient with us and will continue to pursue us, knocking at the doors of our hearts. The pager scene is subtle. God doesn't show up in a flash of lightning, power, and glory; he just persistently pages Bruce.*

• *Can you think of similar examples in your own lives of God subtly "paging" you?*

• *While God will probably never literally page us, he continues to tell us the message he wants us to hear in many subtle ways.*

Just as God persistently pursues Bruce, God pursues his people in the book of Ezekiel.

• *If God pursued his people into exile, what does that tell us about where we can go to get away from God? Is God easily gotten rid of?* Make sure the answers to these two questions highlight that there is no place we can go—even when we're stuck somewhere as a result of our own actions—where God will not come looking for us.

• Say: *You have to want to get rid of God, because his intense love for you will keep him dogging your steps for the entirety of your life span.*

There's one last part of this chapter we need to notice…

• Ask: *Did anyone notice how old Ezekiel is?* Give them a minute to find the answer.

• Explain: *Thirty was the age to begin his ministry as a priest, and yet when Ezekiel turns 30, he's in exile, so he can't start his ministry because there is no temple at which to officiate. But the year he's 30, God shows up and starts him in his ministry as not only a priest, in the sense that he's a messenger to his people, but also as a prophet—one who speaks for God.*

• *Now, the Israelites had been in exile for about five years, and God could have called Ezekiel to be a prophet some other year, but he initiated him into the priesthood exactly when he should have been initiated. What does this tell you about God?* When God calls you to do something, you can be assured it will happen.

• *And it will happen even if stuff around you happens that's completely beyond your control—so much so that it looks like what you thought you were supposed to do will now be impossible.*

Conclude: *So the question never is, "Where is God?" He is there. He is here. And just like God had a call and a plan for Ezekiel, he has a call and a plan for you and me. It's up to us whether we're going to step into that plan. But he's always there, waiting, because just as he was madly in love with the people of Israel, he's madly in love with you and with me and wants a relationship with us.*

And if you think about the majesty of God in this chapter, the fact that this awesome God desperately wants to talk to us, to have a relationship with us, is an amazing thing! And when God is with us, even when things have happened that are completely beyond our control, he can still bring about his plans for our lives, because after all, this is the God, the only true God, and he is powerful enough to take your life and turn it into something beautiful.

CLOSING

Pass out the journaling exercise, **Called to Belong to Jesus Christ**. Encourage your students to spend a few minutes with God praying and journaling. If space permits, have them spread out. Put some meditative music on, and let them have some space to deal with the questions and thoughts this session may have raised. Start playing "Facedown" by Matt Redman (*Facedown*, 2004; you can get the song from iTunes for $0.99) or another reflective song, and then after about 10 minutes, start singing it so they can join in as they finish. (If you plan to sing a song as a group, make sure to provide lyrics.)

JOURNALING: CALLED TO BELONG TO JESUS CHRIST

What sort of "picture" of God did you have before we talked about Ezekiel 1?

Has this chapter changed your view? If so, how?

What does it mean to you that you can't outrun God? To know he's always there?

Read Romans 1:6. What does this verse mean to you after thinking about what we've talked about in this session?

Write to God and tell him what you're thinking right now…

THE WATCHMAN MENTALITY
SESSION 2: EZEKIEL 3:16-27; 1 PETER 2:9; ROMANS 15:16

OVERVIEW

Once we understand the God who has called us, we next need to realize the importance of what he has called us to. This is no easy task, for we are called to be lights, to be watchmen and women for our generation. And many people don't want to see. God has called us not to success, per se, but to be faithful to him. It's going to be difficult, as the allusion to briars, thorns, and scorpions in Ezekiel 2:6 would suggest. However, we are commissioned to remember who has called us, and that "In spite of the turmoil outside, God's servants may be secure in the knowledge that all is well for them in the hands of the ever-present Lord."[2]

SET UP

ACTIVITY

• An obstacle course created out of tables and chairs (Have several blindfolds on hand.)

---

[2] Block, *The Book of Ezekiel*: Chapters 1-24, 161.

MOVIE

• *A Walk to Remember*

SECTION 1: BACKGROUND FOR LEADERS

HOW HARD IS IT TO BE A WATCHMAN?

One night my fiancé (now husband) was backing up his truck along a poorly lit rural road so I could get inside. In the dark he could barely see the edge of the road, and as he backed up, I noticed that a fallen tree had crumbled part of the road away. I thought for a second about yelling that his tire was too close to the edge, but I hesitated because it looked like it would be okay. What I couldn't see was that the road itself was somewhat eroded under the pavement because of the tree falling. The weight of his truck crumbled a little more of the road, and the front tire slipped into the hole left by the tree's roots.

Thankfully, the hole wasn't that deep, so his axle didn't get hung up on the edge of the road, and he was able to switch the truck into four-wheel drive and get it out of the hole without much drama. But as soon as his truck slipped into the hole, you can imagine that I was seriously kicking myself for not trying to warn him the second the thought had flashed through my head. And this wasn't some random stranger, either. This was the man I love, and I didn't react fast enough. Makes me wonder how often I hesitate when it comes to warning other people whom I don't know as well about things that, in the end, will be far more important.

The passages we're looking at in this session all deal with the same thing: the responsibility of the watchman. God appointed Ezekiel as a watchman for his people. A watchman warns of impending danger whether or not the people want to hear the message. After all, who wants their peaceful lives interrupted by the knowledge that they have to do something major to change how they're living?

WILL PEOPLE LISTEN?

In late August of 2005, one of the worst hurricanes to ever come ashore decimated much of New Orleans and many of the surrounding communities extending into three states. New Orleans, of course, got the most coverage because it was the biggest city and the damage in this one area was the most devastating. What happened to New Orleans actually wasn't so much the result of Katrina coming through, but rather the result of not listening to the watchmen and women who warned of what could happen if a hurricane of that force hit the city.

See, most of the damage in the city wasn't caused by the storm itself, even though the storm was terrible. The biggest problem came because the levees failed and flooded a huge portion of the city, and the chaos resulted in residents not getting rescued in a timely fashion. The aftermath will take years to sort out.

But as early as 2002, scientists had come up with a scenario that was disturbingly similar to what actually happened, right down to the number of people they thought would be unable to leave and how people would take refuge in the Superdome and so forth. But the emergency-response systems didn't prepare as if the scenario would take place. Also, engineers had known for some time that the levees wouldn't hold up against a storm with that type of force—but was something done about it? No. So the worst tragedy of the storm was that it was so much worse than it could have been because people failed to hear the cry of the watchmen.

In hindsight of course, I'm sure there are at least a half million people who believe the warnings from the scientists and engineers should have been given more of an audience, but I wonder what the response would have been had those studies gained widespread attention in the years before Katrina. Would people have listened? Would they really have wanted to hear?

Maybe they would have, but it's hard to say. If it was that hard to get across a message of warning about something like a storm, how much harder is it to stand as watchmen and women and try to warn people that they need to make a decision about their eternal destinies and reconsider the way they're living their lives here on earth? With the storm warnings, it's safe to assume that in the future people will take warnings like that more seriously and act to prevent disasters of that nature from wreaking the kind of havoc that Katrina wreaked. But with something as seemingly intangible—at least at first glance—as salvation, it's incredibly difficult to gain an audience. Sometimes when people's worlds get shaken, they're more likely to listen, but before that, when things are going well, it's hard to imagine the kind of damage we saw in New Orleans, and even harder to imagine the consequences and havoc that can be wreaked in the life of someone who doesn't choose to follow Jesus.

BONUS: LEADER DEVOTIONAL THOUGHT—GETTING TO THE WATCHMAN MENTALITY

The end of the passage from Ezekiel 3 is different than anything contained in the other two parallel passages in that it contains an account of the prophet being rendered speechless and unable to move for a season. Ezekiel is to be set apart from the other exiles and unable to speak except for speaking the words of God (verses 26-27). It seems as though this season extends from Ezekiel's call in 593 BC until the sacking of Jerusalem in 587 BC. Ezekiel was to be known only as the mouthpiece of God,[3] and thus he would be unable to speak unless it was God speaking through him. That way, whenever the people heard Ezekiel speaking, they could be sure that God was trying to get their attention.

[3] Allen, *Ezekiel 1-19*, 63.

Talk about an all-encompassing ministry! This call completely interrupts Ezekiel's life and focuses it on the task of proclaiming God's word to the people. Ezekiel's entire life from this point on was to serve as a sign for the people of Israel, whether or not they paid any attention to him.

Now this isn't an endorsement for becoming a workaholic in your ministry. You can be holistic about your life and ministry and be consumed by passion and the message you have to speak, but nowhere does the book suggest that Ezekiel didn't have time to rest. Nor are we to assume that just because we're called to speak God's word that everything we speak *is* God's word. Unfortunately we're all too capable of speaking our own words quite often, since God hasn't bound any of us in our houses and struck us dumb unless it's time to speak about his word.

The point for us to get out of this passage is that this word God is trying to get across is in no way passive. It is a living word, and this living word has a possessive quality about it[4] in that once you answer the call on your life to speak the words of God to his people—if you take that call seriously—the message will overtake you. It'll get into you in ways you never dreamed possible as you study God's Word, and then you'll feel compelled to share your findings. In that way, the Word has a hold on you, and those who're that swept away by God's Word will find themselves sharing it in both verbal and nonverbal ways and thus living the lives of watchmen and women.

SECTION 2: MAKING IT LIVE FOR YOUR STUDENTS

STARTING GAME

• Have the obstacle course set up before your students arrive.

• Number your students into two groups at random.

• Line up each group on opposite sides of the obstacle course.

• One group will serve as the "watchmen" and help students from the other group across the room. NOTE: If you have a large group, you may need to set up two obstacle courses in different rooms or simply select several volunteers to do this, and have it serve more as an illustration.

• Blindfold two students from the first group.

• Designate one student to be guided across the room so he knows that the vocal commands are for him.

• Have one student from the second group guide one of the blindfolded students across the room, using voice commands. IMPORTANT: Make sure the kids go slowly, and perhaps have an adult leader shadow the blindfolded student who isn't getting the voice commands in case she loses her balance or steps too fast and trips. If you have younger kids, you may want to shadow both of them.

---

4 Vawter and Hoppe, *Ezekiel: A New Heart*, 36.

INTRODUCTION

Call the kids together and pray for your time together. If you'd like to encourage a student to pray, perhaps having him or her read a prayer like the following may help the student get into the mode of praying in public.

Almighty God, heavenly Father, thank you for this time to come together and look at what your Word has to say to us today. Teach us by the power of your Holy Spirit what it is we need to learn from you. Open our hearts so we can understand and absorb your truth. In the name of Jesus we pray, amen.

The following is a story that happened to me, written in the first person. You can use this, or tell the truck story from the Background for Leaders section. Or you could discuss the warnings given before Hurricane Katrina hit New Orleans, also highlighted in the Background section. If you want to use the following story, you can tell it as though it happened to a friend of yours (hey, we're venturing through the book of Ezekiel together—we must be friends by now!); or if you've experienced a similar situation, where someone tried to warn you about something and you didn't want to listen, then use your own story instead.

For several years after I [one of my friends] started driving, my dad [his or her dad, okay, you get the picture] would always tell me I followed other cars too closely—especially on the freeway. At the time, I was living in Los Angeles, and leaving enough space between the cars was difficult, since people would zoom into the gaps you left, soon eating up all the extra space they tell you in Driver's Ed to leave. Well, I was sick of people always getting in front of me, so I started following other cars closer than I should have, and when my dad rode with me, he was like, "Pull back!" After a couple of close calls, even a nagging little voice inside me told me I should stop following so close, or I was going to have an accident. And yet, even with my dad's warning and the nagging little voice inside me, I didn't listen. I just didn't think it was ever going to happen to me. Until one day, the traffic stopped suddenly in front of me during a split second when I was slightly distracted by something on the other side of the road, and I couldn't stop fast enough. I plowed into the car in front of me, and I remember one of the first things that went through my mind was, *I can't believe that just happened to me.* Of course, it wasn't like I hadn't had ample warning, but I just never believed it could happen to me.

Now, do you suppose if my dad had known for sure I wouldn't listen to him until it was too late, he wouldn't have tried to warn me anyway? I don't think so. I think he would have still done everything in his power to try to warn me to change my driving habits.

DIGGING IN: WHAT DOES IT MEAN TO BE A WATCHMAN?

Have several volunteers each read several verses of Ezekiel 3:16-27. Then say: *Just like the dad in the story tried to warn his daughter about her driving habits, Ezekiel was called to warn the people of Israel.*

• *Going back to our game, which person had an easier time of getting through the maze?* Hopefully when you played your game, the person who had someone to guide him or her through the maze made it through faster and didn't trip over much.

• *Why was it easier for the person with the guide to get through the maze?*

• *What was the job of the guide in the game?* Make sure you summarize people's answers, emphasizing that the guide's job is to make sure that the person he or she is guiding doesn't run into anything.

• Explain: *That's the role of a watchman. A watchman is a person who wants to keep people from tripping over stuff. And in life, we are to warn people even if they don't listen. After all, some will listen. And some won't. Whether or not it seems like most people listen to us is not what being a watchman is about. It's not a popularity contest. It's a call to be faithful. Now, what does that look like…?*

THE LIFE OF A WATCHMAN

Before the lesson, mark 1 Peter 2:9 and Romans 15:16 in two different Bibles. Pass the marked passages to two students, and have them read the 1 Peter passage and then the Romans passage. Explain the life of a watchman by saying something like this: *The verse from 1 Peter tells us we are a royal priesthood. Romans 15:16 tells us what that means—the priestly duty is to proclaim the gospel of God. In preaching the gospel to the Gentiles, Paul sees himself functioning as a priest.*

• *Based on these verses, what role are we all called to?* Priests.

• *And what is our function?* Proclaiming the gospel.

• *As we move through Ezekiel's story, he will show us that this call to proclaim the gospel means more than just preaching—it involves your entire life.*

MOVIE CLIP: *A WALK TO REMEMBER—*A QUIET WATCHMAN

Play the clip. START [00:16:06] STOP [00:18:10] (Bus scene)

• *What assumptions does Landon make in this scene?* He assumes he knows all about her…

• *What does he base those assumptions on?* They've gone to the same school since they were little children.

• *How does Jamie react to Landon's assumptions?* Rather then being angry with his view of her, she merely tells him not to think he knows her.

• *Does she change anything about her life?* She continues on with her life exactly as she had been doing before.

• *Why are Landon and Jamie on that bus together?* Landon comes into contact with Jamie because they end up tutoring students together. Landon was there because he got community-service hours for being involved in causing injury to another student in a dare. In contrast, Jamie was tutoring students to help them.

• *How does Landon start treating Jamie after this?* Realizing that she tutors students just to help them turns her into a bit of a mystery to Landon. Later in the film, she becomes an example and finally a love interest.

• *How do other students in this film view her life at the beginning? At the end?*

• Explain: *Eventually her life and the way she lived it in spite of her illness have an impact on a number of students at her school. She didn't talk a lot to her classmates, but it became very clear where she stood and what she stood for. This is a good example of living a "watchman" sort of life. No matter what people think, we can boldly stand our ground and proclaim our message even if they never listen to anything we say.*

Conclude: *We have to remember our relationship with God comes first. This watchman deal is an inside-out sort of thing. If the relationship isn't there, good works mean nothing. Only by having a real relationship with God can we be authentic watchmen and watchwomen for our time.*

And when our relationship with God is our first priority, then our whole lives will turn into visible messages that there is another way to live. When our whole lives are messages, both our words and actions will be warning people to turn from the evil that will lead to much destruction in their lives and ultimately, to death. We will be living messages of hope and life in a world where chaos and destruction are the ultimate ends of a lifestyle without God. That's the watchman mentality.

CLOSING

Pass out the journaling exercise, **What's It Worth?** Encourage the students to spend a few minutes with God praying and journaling. If space permits, have them spread out. Put some meditative music on, and let them have some time to deal with the questions and thoughts this session may have raised.

JOURNALING: WHAT'S IT WORTH?

What lifestyle adjustments have you made so your relationship with God will be closer?

What kinds of adjustments are you willing to make?

If someone looked at your life, would that person be able to tell you're a Christian?

Write to God and tell him what you're thinking right now…

OVERVIEW

What was the purpose of all these dramatic signs against Israel? God was going to great lengths to get his children's attention. Even though Israel had sinned greatly against God, he loved her so much he was trying to get her to come back. How far will God have to go to get your attention?

SET UP

ACTIVITY: LAYING SIEGE TO JERUSALEM

• For options, read the Laying Siege to the City of Jerusalem section in Making It Live for Your Students. Proceed according to the instructions in that section.

OPTION ONE: BATTERING-RAM CONTEST

• One brick

- A large metal baking pan
- At least four cups of regular dirt
- ½ cup to a cup of water
- 50 to 60 Popsicle sticks or other wooden building material
- Pipe cleaners
- Glue guns
- Glue sticks
- String
- Two folding tables in the front of the room on either side of where you'll be presenting the lesson
- Several large plastic trash bags
- Plenty of paper towels for cleanup
- Candy for prizes

Cover one of the tables with the trash bags, and place the metal baking pan in the center. Pour the dirt into the pan, making sure room is left between the top of the dirt and the top of the pan to prevent spilling. Moisten the dirt. It should be moist enough that you can pat it firm, but not muddy. Place the brick in the center of the pan.

OPTION TWO: SIGNS AGAINST JERUSALEM

- Several plastic toy battering rams perhaps from a medieval play set
- One brick or cardboard box on which you've drawn a city
- One large iron skillet (or frying pan)
- Two folding tables pushed together in the front of the room

MOVIE

- *Bruce Almighty*

SECTION 1: BACKGROUND FOR LEADERS

HOW HARDHEADED CAN THEY BE?

It's entirely possible that as we're reading the book of Ezekiel—especially passages such as these—we're thinking, *How can these people* not *be paying attention to what God is trying to say?* After all, God is going to great lengths to get his people's attention, and the things God says will happen to them if they don't pay attention are serious indeed. In fact, if we read through this section beginning with chapter 4 on through to the end of chapter 7, we encounter statements made by God that sound downright horrible. These types of statements are part of the reason why the book of Ezekiel is often overlooked when we teach the Old Testament. There's stuff in here we just don't want to explain or deal with.

And yet, even these parts we don't like to read in Ezekiel are explained in Ezekiel 7:27, where, in the second part of the verse, God says, "I will deal with them according to their conduct, and by their own standards I will judge them." Here, "Ezekiel affirms that the criteria for the Lord's justice mirror the prior commitments of the people."[5] Notice that the rest of the world isn't living in relationship with God, and yet God isn't judging them. He's judging Israel because she made a commitment to him—a covenant—and the Israelites were no longer keeping this covenant.

ARE WE FORGETTING SOMETHING HERE?

The Israelites forgot that God wasn't just there to defeat their enemies, send them rain when they needed it, or handle whatever else happened to be confronting them at the moment. This was a covenant—a relationship—and the people of Israel weren't living their part of the covenant.

Imagine trying to do that in a marriage or a dating relationship. Try getting your significant other to do all the good stuff for you while you go off and fool around with other people. This is the language God uses in Ezekiel 6:9 when he says, "How I was crushed by their wanton heart that turned away from me, and their wanton eyes that turned after their idols" (NRSV).

But here God isn't just a jealous lover trying to get his beloved's attention. No, God had to act against Israel in order to save his own reputation. That might sound incredibly selfish, but when we think about why Israel was set apart to be God's chosen people, it makes sense.

Right at the beginning of the first covenant God made with Abraham, God tells Abraham he will bless him and make his name great—not so that Abraham can sit around and enjoy having a great name, but so he "will be a blessing" and so "all peoples on earth will be blessed through" him (Genesis 12:2-3). The point of Abraham's calling and the birth of this special nation was so all people—note, not all the people of Israel, but of the earth—could be blessed. The nation of Israel was supposed to be a sign for the rest of the world of how great God is so the rest of the world could hear about this God and choose to come to know him. This is the idea behind Ezekiel 5:5 when God says, "This is Jerusalem; I have set her in the center of the nations, with countries all around her" (NRSV).

But "she has rebelled against my ordinances and my statutes" (verse 6, NRSV), and thus Israel wasn't living any differently from the surrounding nations. Rather, she had become "more wicked than the nations and the countries all around her" (verse

5 New Interpreter's Study Bible, comment on Ezekiel 7:27.

6, NRSV). There was no way the light of God could shine through her actions when Israel was doing all kinds of horrible things. We're not just talking sacrifices to idols—the Israelites had gotten as far as sacrificing infants to these idols (16:20; 20:31) among all their numerous abominations. As commentators point out, "Israel did not witness to the nations. Israel disregarded Yahweh's ordinances and statutes. She had even surpassed the Gentiles in sinning against them, adopting the way of the nations instead of the LORD's."[6] And so God must act, or else none of the other nations will be able to see that this God is different from any other god they've ever known.

And so God allows his people to be carried off into exile. But as we note in session 1 (and will get further into in session 5), this is a God who follows his people into exile and continues to seek their attention. God pursues his people through a series of sign acts, which we find in the passages we're looking at for this week's session.

NOTE: In case one of your kids brings it up, be aware of the disturbing imagery in Ezekiel 5 of parents eating children and children eating parents. If it comes up, explain that this refers to the conditions of a city under siege. When the whole city was out of food and starving to death, people would often cook and eat the people who had recently died in order to try to stay alive. (Yeah, gotta love the hard-to-swallow images in the Bible…pun intended!) If you think your group will read the whole passage, you may want to just cover it in the midst of your discussion on sign acts and point out that God is warning about the horrible things that will happen if repentance doesn't occur.

SECTION 2: MAKING IT LIVE FOR YOUR STUDENTS

INTRODUCTION

MOVIE CLIP: *BRUCE ALMIGHTY—ASKING FOR A SIGN*

Play the clip.
START [00:21:03] STOP [00:23:20]

• *Ask: What was the significance of the truck full of signs?*

• *What did you think about Bruce's reaction?*

• *Do you believe we ever react that way when God is trying to get our attention?*

• Summarize: *A lot of times it seems we humans are overquick to blame God for not sending us a "sign," when quite often the answer to our prayer is right in front of us. In this clip Bruce wants to hear from God, so he prays, "God, show me a sign." A truck*

6 Vawter and Hoppe, *Ezekiel: A New Heart*, 48.

full of signs pulls in front of him. He asked for one. He got a whole truckload. But what does he do? He pulls around it in frustration and resumes his talk with God.

The passage we're looking at today is a lot like this scene between Bruce and God, only the scene in Ezekiel happens between God and a whole nation of people.

DIGGING IN: LAYING SIEGE TO THE CITY OF JERUSALEM

Have four volunteers read two verses each of Ezekiel 4:1-8. Then proceed with the illustration. Depending on the size of your group, you have two different options for laying siege to the city of Jerusalem. Before you start, explain:

• Ezekiel portrays the upcoming siege of Jerusalem using a brick and models of current siege weapons. These included earthworks or siege ramps to roll the battering rams against the walls of the city. The battering rams would have been built out of wood, on wheels, and covered with wicker shields.

• The primary feature, of course, was the metal ramming rod, which soldiers would run up against a city wall between the stones (aiming at the mortar) and then move from side to side to loosen one of the large city stones so the wall would partially collapse and the soldiers could then rush inside.

OPTION ONE: BATTERING-RAM CONTEST

• Complete the instructions under Set Up.

• Make piles of Popsicle sticks, pipe cleaners, string, and several glue sticks near one of the glue guns.

• Plug the glue guns in before the students arrive, and make sure you keep the students away from them, since they'll be getting hot.

• After reading Ezekiel 4, create teams of four to five people each.

• Instruct students to create a battering ram out of the materials provided and build a siege ramp out of the dirt going up to the brick.

• If you have too large a group to build siege ramps, then you can leave that part out.

• The first team to complete a believable battering ram wins.

OPTION TWO: SIGNS AGAINST JERUSALEM

• Prepare a volunteer in advance to play Ezekiel while you discuss the significance of Ezekiel's actions. Have the volunteer set up battering rams around the brick or box that represents the city. Then after he or she finishes, the volunteer can climb up on one of the tables and lie down on one side with the frying pan between the city and him or her.

NOTE: While discussing this chapter, be careful of a couple of things. First, be sure to completely explain why God is judging Israel, emphasizing that this is occurring not because God is vindictive, but because God wants people to be in relationship with him. Next, make sure you don't make it sound as though God is going to zap individual people if they're a "bad witness." That's not the point, but it'd be easy to go there if you get overly literal trying to make a parallel between the individual Christian and the nation of Israel. Remember, the point is that God cares so much that even after Israel has run off and cheated on him, God's still trying to get her attention and win her back.

Reread Ezekiel 4:1-8 yourself.

• Ask: *What is the point of God getting Ezekiel to do these weird things?* These sign acts are God pleading with his people to turn and repent. They're dramatic performances aimed at getting the people's attention and explaining to them what's going to happen.

• *How long does it say that Ezekiel lay on his side?* Three hundred and ninety days on the left and 40 days on the right. This is more than a year!

• Explain: *It's possible that Ezekiel would have been lying on his side for a time period every day, while going home at night to sleep and do his regular chores. It's also possible that God miraculously enabled him to lie there for a very long time. Either way, it's hard to miss this dude lying in the street every day! "Hey Ezekiel, what are you doing?" "Still lying on my side..."*

• *What does the iron pan in verse 3 represent?* The iron plate or griddle represents that once Israel gets so far that God has to bring the Babylonians in to take out the city, there's no stopping it. Jerusalem will fall if Israel doesn't repent now.

• Explain: *God can't ignore what they've done and what they're continuing to do. But this isn't a God who haphazardly fires lightning bolts from heaven when he's angry at his people! This is a God who grieves over the wayward hearts of his people and how they've cheated on him and played him falsely. And even after all that, God follows Israel to where they are in exile and pleads with them to please pay attention now so things don't get even worse than they already are.*

• *Several times in the next couple of chapters, you find the phrase: "They will know that I am the LORD." Why do you suppose God is so interested in getting people to know that he is the LORD?* God is always looking to draw people to himself. When we see God for who he really is, then we have the opportunity to decide whether or not to follow him.

• *In several places, God seems concerned with his reputation among the other nations that were around Israel. Why do you think God cares what people think of him? Is God vain?* God cares that people see who he really is. He can't let a false image of himself get out there because then people won't be able to choose whether or not they want to be in relationship with him.

Explain: *You could look at exile itself as one big sign act. It's a purposeful action, an attempt to get the people's attention. But the people have a messed-up view of God. They think God will bring them back to the land because he has something to prove. The people think God has to prove to the other nations and their false gods that they can't come in and mess with God's land like that. They think the point is that their God is bigger than the other gods, and thus they are safe in the land that belongs to him. And he will keep them safe to prove his might to the other gods.*

But this God—our God—is never concerned with things or places. He's concerned about people's hearts. While he will act for the sake of his name, it's not to prove his might in his land; it's to draw people to have a relationship with him because that's what God's about—relationship.

Conclude: *The moral of the story then, when it comes to these sign acts, is, "How far will God have to go to get your attention?" See, God will go to dramatic lengths to get your attention so you can get to know him on a personal level and then walk in his ways—not because he likes to impose a bunch of random rules on people, but because his ways are full of real life and joy and peace; and they are good. God will never force anyone to do anything. He may jump up and down, yell, and go through all sorts of measures to try to attract our attention, court us, and try to get us to give him a chance, but God will never force us.*

Far from being the bizarre and ominous deeds these sign acts may have resembled when we first looked at them, they are dramatic demonstrations of God's undying love for us, as well as shining examples of God's hope in humankind that we will turn and listen to him.

CLOSING

Pass out the journaling exercise, **Our Lives in Focus**. Encourage students to spend a few minutes with God praying and journaling. If space permits, have them spread out. Put some meditative music on, and let them have some time to deal with the questions and thoughts this session may have raised.

JOURNALING: OUR LIVES IN FOCUS

What are some of the things you've thought in the past about why God does some of the things he does?

What difference does it make to you to understand that God puts having a relationship with people as his very first priority? Does that change some of the things you thought about why God acts the way he does?

How important is your relationship with God, in relation to the other things that are important to you in your life?

If a stranger looked at your life, how would this person rate your relationship with God? What if a friend looked at your life?

What are some things God has done to get your attention? What was your response? Talk with God about what obstacles might be in the way of your relationship with him.

DRIVING GOD AWAY

SESSION 4: EZEKIEL 8 (ESPECIALLY VERSE 6); PSALM 139:23-24; ROMANS 12:1

OVERVIEW

God is all powerful; however, how much of that power is shown in your life depends on how much you're letting God do. God won't force himself into places he's not wanted, nor will God stay where he's no longer welcome. Are there things in your life that are pushing God away?

SET UP

This session contains a detailed walk through the temple, which will probably be unfamiliar to most of your students. For some good pictures, surf to www.wikipedia. org and type "Solomon's Temple" in the search box.

ACTIVITY

• Something you can use to make a visible list on a wall (such as a whiteboard, chalkboard, or newsprint flip chart)

• This illustration from Wikipedia drawn on the board large enough for everyone to see (Remember, a courtyard with gates would be around the temple, and the altar would be to the right of where the brazen Sea is depicted. See the Wikipedia article for a detailed description.)

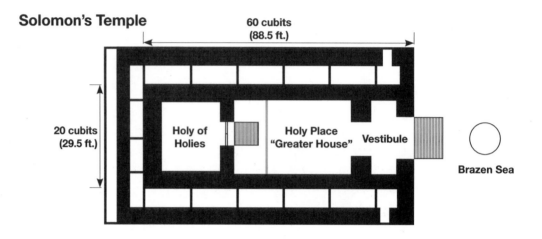

Solomon's Temple

MOVIE

• *Bruce Almighty*

SECTION 1: BACKGROUND FOR LEADERS

WHAT DOES GOD SEE?

You'd think that after having been in exile, and then having the siege and fall of the beloved capital city portrayed to them, the Israelites would pay some attention to Ezekiel's words. After all, it's not as though prophets were a foreign notion to the Jewish nation. Prophets had emerged all through Israel's history as one of God's most prominent means of getting his word to the people. So this prophet doing sign acts in the midst of them was a formula Israel should have readily recognized.

One fine day in September—September 18, to be precise—of 592 BC, Ezekiel is said to have been visited with yet another vision of the glory of the LORD. This is 14 months after the first vision, presumably during the time he is completing the sign acts of lying on his side to bear the punishment of both Israel and Judah. This would lend credence to the idea that he lay on his side for a period of time each day during the proscribed sign act, rather then being immobilized for the duration. Ezekiel 8 opens in his house, with the elders of Judah looking to him for some sort of prophecy or word from the LORD. No doubt the sign acts had gotten their attention at least to the point that they wanted to hear just what this prophet had to say.

While these men are sitting in front of Ezekiel, the hand of the LORD comes suddenly on him, and he has a vision. Since the men are sitting right there in front of him and this is called a vision, all the transporting that goes on in the next few paragraphs is most likely some sort of out-of-body experience—and a very poignant one. Ezekiel is transported to Jerusalem so the LORD can show him the case against Israel.

THE CASE AGAINST ISRAEL

Ezekiel 8 walks us through the temple, starting with the idol set up in one of the entrance gates. Then Ezekiel digs through a wall to discover 70 images, with 70 leaders of Israel each serving as a sort of "priest" in each individual shrine. This number recalls the number of leaders of the house of Israel from when Moses was in the desert (Exodus 24:1-9; Numbers 11:16; 24-25[7]), so it represents a significant portion of Israelites here, including one named Jaazaniah, the son of Shaphan, from a prominent house in Israel, which possibly means the perversion was spread throughout the entire house of Israel. In fact, Jaazaniah means, "Yahweh listens"[8] and possibly reflects his parents longing for the voice of Yahweh. Yet even though his own name reminds him that Yahweh is indeed still present, Jaazaniah is in the midst of these men, offering up incense to engraved idols on the walls of this secret temple room, thinking, "The LORD does not see us; the LORD has forsaken the land" (Ezekiel 8:12).

Then the LORD takes Ezekiel and shows him women at the north gate of the temple practicing a mourning ritual for a deity called Tammuz, banished to the underworld by his wife. This resulted in yearly lamentation for his death, and this is what these women are doing in the north gate of Yahweh's temple. Do they think Yahweh is absent, and thus use this lamentation as mourning because they believe Yahweh and Tammuz are one and the same and have suffered the same fate? Who knows? The point is "Ezekiel observes the people of Jerusalem replacing the vital worship of the living God with lamentations for the dead."[9]

The last scene Ezekiel is shown in his vision is a group of men in the inner court of the temple. Remember, the holiest place in the temple was in the innermost part, so as you go from outer to inner, you are moving to holier ground. And here, not in the innermost, but still within the inner wall, is a group of men between the porch and the altar, bowing down to the sun. In order to do this, they have to turn their backs to the temple (verse 16), and thus they are both literally and figuratively turning their backs on God.

DRIVING GOD AWAY

Here's the kicker. You might think, *Well, maybe the Israelites didn't know any better. I mean, they didn't have the benefit of the complete canon of Scripture like we do. They were confused.* But this entire generation would have been around for the reforms of Josiah when he found the book of the law (2 Kings 22), which would be Deuteronomy, and did away with all the idol worship. That happened right about the

[7] Allen, *Ezekiel 1-19*, 143.
[8] Block, *The Book of Ezekiel: Chapters 1-24*, 290.
[9] Ibid., 296.

time Ezekiel would have been born, or about 622 BC. It's now 592 BC, so the initial exile was only about 24 or 25 years after the reforms of Josiah. In those 20-some-odd years, these people had completely reformed after recognizing the error of their idol-worshiping ways, but then managed to somehow forget all of that and go right back at it, to the point where they took themselves out from under God's hand of protection and got themselves exiled.

Sadly, the exile of their fellow citizens didn't cause those who stayed behind to re-examine their own lives. In fact, their behavior simply continued to worsen, until their idolatrous ways resulted in the glory of the LORD departing from the temple (Ezekiel 10:18-22) and then from the city altogether (11:22-25). The Israelites had effectively driven God from their midst. And believe me, this took some doing! If you read through the Old Testament, it's one cycle after another of the Israelites falling away, being called back to repentance, falling away, coming back, and so on. This wasn't the first time Israel had decided to mess around with other gods. Only this time they weren't paying attention to Yahweh's efforts to get their attention and win them back. They had decided he was gone for good, and they were off to fend for themselves.

If it can be said that God won't force people to follow him, then it can also be said that God doesn't make it hard to find him, either. God's always there, waiting, watching, trying to get people to realize who he is so he can be in relationship with them. It's God's nature to love, and God wants people on whom he can pour out his love. But if someone turns his back on God and chooses to replace God with things that get in the middle of their relationship, then God allows himself to be pushed away because, again, he doesn't force himself on people.

NATIONS AND INDIVIDUALS

Here, as in other parts of this book, it's helpful to note that the way God deals with the nation of Israel is not representative of how he deals with individuals, per se. God isn't going to kill you because you have idols in your heart, although the paths those idols lead you down very well may. This is an important point to note and keep in perspective.

SECTION 2: MAKING IT LIVE FOR YOUR STUDENTS

INTRODUCTION/ILLUSTRATION

• Divide your group into smaller groups of perhaps 10 people each. (If your youth group is very large, then just prior to giving your talk, simply tell them to stand up and arrange themselves in groups of about 10 students.)

• Then tell them to pick one person from each group who will do whatever you tell them to do.

• Have the groups send that one person up front and then make a circle (more or less).

• Take the volunteers aside and tell them you're going to put them in the center of their group with no explanation to the rest of the group.

• Tell your volunteers to wait a few seconds or so after you say, "We're ready," and then begin to make all sorts of disgusting noises (example: coughing, sneezing, snorting, making it sound like they're about to spit—but not really). They could even do weird behavior (rocking back and forth, moaning, flailing their arms (once people have started moving away) or walk up to people, get in their personal space, and try to stare them down or something. Think about what will work with your group…if you have a lot of staring contests, then that might not make someone back up, and so on).

• Send the volunteers back to their groups, and have them stand in the middle so the other people can see them. IMPORTANT: Don't say anything else to the rest of the group like "don't move" or "stand close to the person" or something like that because the point is to get them to move. If they're standing in a circle, they should be close enough to the person to get the desired result.

• When the volunteers are prepped and the groups are formed, give the cue, "We're ready," and then wait for the weirdness to begin. Sounds from other groups ought to help as people will start looking around, and they should begin to move away from the center of their group, because who wants to be near someone doing disgusting things?

Ask your students: *Why did you move away?* They will likely explain how they don't want to be near someone doing all that weird stuff…

DIGGING IN: THE SECRET ROOM

Read Ezekiel 8 with your students. Select a volunteer (either a student or an adult) who can read effectively and somewhat dramatically (without overdoing it). Have the students close their eyes and picture the different places this chapter takes them. When you're finished, tell them to:

• *Picture the innermost room of your hearts, the place with all your secrets, desires, and longings…*

• *Ask: If someone were to dig a hole into that room and get a look around, what would that person see?*

• *What would that person be able to tell about your life?*

• *What do you value?*

• *Would you really want someone to see all the things you're thinking about right now?*

• *Would you want God to see?*

• *Do you really know that God can still see you, or do you sort of hope there's a place deep, dark, and secret enough he can't?*

IN BED WITH ANOTHER LOVER

Go to your illustration of Solomon's temple and point out the various parts you've labeled. Tell your students: *Starting at Ezekiel 8:3, let's make a list of the things Ezekiel saw.* As your students list them, draw or write a representation on your illustration. Or if you have creative students in the group who can stay on task, have a student volunteer or two come up and draw representations of what Ezekiel saw (this needs to be done fairly quickly, though).

After you have a representation of everything in the vision, say: *The first thing Ezekiel sees is a statue set up in the temple gate, "…the idol that provokes to jealousy…"* (verse 3).

• *First, someone tell me what an idol is…* Summarize the definitions the students come up with as "something that takes the place of God."

• *Right off the top of your head, why do you think this idol is described as "the idol that provokes to jealousy"?*

• *What kind of reaction do you think God is having when he sees this idol?* This image indeed provokes a violent reaction on the part of Yahweh, a reaction that's like a spouse coming home unexpectedly and finding his or her wife or husband in bed with another.

• *Israel and God were in a covenant, a lot like marriage is supposed to be a covenant. Based on that, why would you say God is having this kind of reaction?* This violation was taking place in the temple—the very place where Yahweh had promised to make his dwelling with his people. If your students don't get that, you may want to ask: *What was the purpose of the temple?* Then draw out why God is having this reaction from there. The idol in the temple is like Israel cheating on God.

Depending on the age and maturity of your group, you may or may not want to use the following mental exercise. (I did this with one group, and I had one middle school boy who couldn't get it out of his head for the rest of the night. It will, however, get their attention.)

• Say: *Picture you're 20 years older than you are right now. This should put you somewhere in your 30s.*

• *You've been married for about five years, maybe have a couple of kids.*

• *You get off from work early one day, and you head home, hoping to change clothes and relax, maybe take your spouse out to dinner since you've got some extra time on your hands.*

• *You hurry into the house and head straight for your bedroom to change.*

• *But when you walk in, you discover that your spouse is cheating on you...in your bed.*

• *How would you feel?* After calming down some of the reactions you may get, go on to say:

• *The most blatant in-your-face adultery is that which takes place in bed at home! The very place that should be dedicated to building up the marriage—the very representation of that intimacy—has been violated, along with the covenant of marriage. This is the very thing Israel was doing in the house of her God. And she thought he no longer could see...*

Return to the text by saying: *The* Lord *asks Ezekiel, "Do you see what they are doing—the utterly detestable things the house of Israel is doing here, things that will drive me far from my sanctuary?" (verse 6). How would you define* sanctuary? A place of refuge.

This was supposed to be a place where people would come to encounter the true and living God, and yet here they had turned it into a place where they cheated on God by worshiping other gods. Again, imagine the sanctity and sanctuary of your home torn completely apart by the intrusion of another person into your marital bed. What would that do to you? To your relationship with your spouse? This is the seriousness of the consequences of Israel's actions here. And it gets worse.

MULTIPLE LOVERS IN SECRET

Say: *Someone tell me what happens in verse 8.* Ezekiel is instructed to dig through a hole in the wall that he sees. Say: *How Ezekiel digs through a temple wall is irrelevant. The point is that he's accessing a secret place and spying on the activity inside.* Point to your drawing and show where some of the side rooms would be. The room Ezekiel is looking into is some side room of the temple.

Ezekiel finds all sorts of terrible and despicable things engraved on the walls. And he finds 70 leaders of Jerusalem worshiping these engravings. This number would represent a significant number of the leaders in Jerusalem and probably show that most of Jerusalem had turned away from God and was worshiping idols.

Okay, in verse 14, the Lord *takes Ezekiel and shows him women at the north gate of the temple who are practicing a mourning ritual for a deity called Tammuz who was killed by his wife. These women were practicing a yearly mourning ritual for a dead god. Besides the fact that they were focusing on another god, why do you suppose God was upset enough about their actions to point this out?* Instead of worshiping the true and living God, they are mourning a dead god who wasn't even real.

And yet it gets even worse than this!

• *The fourth scene in verse 16 shows Ezekiel a group of men in the inner court of the temple. (Remember, the holiest place in the temple was in the innermost part, so as you go from outer to inner, you are moving to holier ground. And here, not in the innermost, but still within the inner wall, is a group of men between the porch and the altar, bowing down to the sun.)* Now, point to the area on the drawing where these men would be and draw a sun on the right side of the picture.

• Ask: *What's significant about the direction these men are facing?* In order to face the sun in the east, they had to turn their backs to the temple (also verse 16), and thus they were both literally and figuratively turning their backs on God.

How could they do that right there in the middle of God's house? Yahweh's temple? The one place of all that should have reminded them of who *they were and* whose *they were they had turned into a place where they committed adultery with other gods.*

Okay, so somebody help me summarize: What kinds of things were disgusting to God in this chapter? We're talking multiple betrayals, adultery, and things that led to injustice and mistreatment of people, human sacrifice, and things that were just unbelievably disgusting to God. *Remember the sign acts from last week? God tries to get Israel's attention time and time again, and what do they do? They ignore him! Turn their backs on him! Go right on doing what they've been doing and adding more and more stuff into the mix. And by doing that, they drive God away.*

MOVIE CLIP: *BRUCE ALMIGHTY*—HOW TO DRIVE AWAY SOMEONE YOU LOVE

Play the clip.
START [01:04:35] STOP [01:07:03]

• Ask: *What does Bruce do wrong in this scene?* His main fault was not pushing Susan away when she tries to kiss him.

• *What is the result in his relationship with Grace?* It is the deathblow to his relationship with Grace.

• Summarize: *Now, his other actions in the film had driven her away, too, but it's the fact that she thought he had betrayed her and was unfaithful to her even just in his heart or with his lips that caused such a reaction from her. If her reaction was that severe with that, imagine knowing that the person you love has betrayed you multiple times with different people and continues to do it. That's what God is trying to get across in this chapter as he shows Ezekiel all the different things going on in the temple.*

LIVING SACRIFICES

Pass a student a Bible with Romans 12:1 marked in it, and have the student read that verse aloud. Say: *In Romans 12:1, Paul urges us to offer our bodies as living sacrifices that are holy and pleasing to God. If we're living sacrifices, then everything we do can be evaluated from the standpoint of whether or not it's glorifying to God.*

Say: *What sort of things take up big pieces of our time?* As the students call out ideas, write a list of the things that take up our time. (If there's space on your board to do this without erasing the drawing of the temple, then leave it up.)

When you finish the list, ask the following questions. You may want to leave these open for reflection and not look for actual answers. To facilitate that, you could say: "Think about these questions," and then leave significant pauses for the students to examine their own lives.

• *Where is our energy and time getting offered up?*

• *Is it in service to God, doing things that are glorifying to him?*

• *Or is it getting offered up more often than not to things that wouldn't be glorifying to him?*

• *If we break down Ezekiel's vision in these terms for us, the secret room is our hearts. How many shrines do we have there?*

• *Or is there just one throne for the living God?*

• *If we have multiple shrines and multiple things that aren't glorifying to God going on simultaneously, it begins to push God out. And if we keep that up, we can push God to a place where we're out from under his protection in our lives.*

Conclude: *Now what does that mean? Do we all need to go join a monastic order so we can focus on God 24/7?* No. *We can serve God in whatever vocation he has called us to, and that doesn't mean just vocational ministry. The question is, who is ultimately on the throne of our hearts? Is it God? Or do we have a bunch of stuff vying for attention in our secret places? Are there sins we've rationalized as not that bad, or that we're in some way trying to make ourselves feel better about? No sin, once we become aware of it, can be left alone. At the instant we become aware of it, we must turn it over to God and with his help begin walking away from that sin, so we'll no longer be dragged down by it or made subject to it. Otherwise, we're effectively burning incense at foreign shrines, and bit by bit we'll begin to push God out of our lives.*

This isn't a call to become paranoid. God brings things that need to be dealt with in our lives to the surface gradually because we couldn't handle everything at once. So, if the question is, Do I have stuff in my life that needs to be dealt with? *The answer is, yes. But if the question is whether or not you're aware of it, the answer depends on whether or not you're paying attention to the latest thing God's trying to work out of your life. Maybe it's a bad habit you've fallen into that's sort of nagging at you. Notice for Israel it's a downward spiral. She doesn't instantly get to the place where she's driven God away. Rather, it's after God's done everything conceivable to get her attention that God's finally driven out by her refusal to hear him. And this is the call this passage has for us. It's a warning that we can actually drive God away. But it's also a call to examine our lives and see if there's a place where we've been missing God's tugging on our hearts to deal with something in our lives standing in the way of our relationships with him.*

The way to avoid letting sin go unacknowledged in our lives is to pray as the psalmist did: "Search me, O God, and know my heart; test me and know my anxious thoughts. See if there is any offensive way in me, and lead me in the way everlasting" (Psalm 139:23-24).

CLOSING

Pass out the journaling exercise, **Which Doors to Open**. Have your students open their Bibles to Psalm 139:23-24. Encourage them to spend a few minutes with God praying and journaling. If space permits, have them spread out. Put some meditative music on, and let them have some time to deal with the questions and thoughts this session may have raised.

When they've finished, bring them back together and close in a song of dedication, one that speaks of offering up one's life to the LORD. In your closing words, remind them that God wants to weed these things out of our lives because they form barriers in our relationships with him, and the closer we get to God—the more in tune with him we are—the better it gets, even when things are difficult.

JOURNALING: WHICH DOORS TO OPEN

Read Psalm 139:23-24.

Am I willing to let God into every region of my heart/life?

Is there anything I already know is in my life that's not glorifying to God and is causing a barrier?

Am I willing to let God bring things to my attention that I won't like and will have to work on with him?

Write to God and tell him what you're thinking right now…

OVERVIEW

The Israelites have not only pushed God away, but even in exile they don't respond to his call to return to him. God has gone to great lengths to get their attention as we've seen—not the least of which is the exile itself. However, this isn't a God who capriciously sends his people into exile; this is a God who accompanies his people into exile. He goes with them and tries to bring them back. And even when they're unresponsive, God still reveals to Ezekiel that he already has a plan in place to restore them. There's nowhere Israel can go where God can't follow and find them. Regardless of the mess you've gotten yourself into, God is right there calling, waiting, and watching for you to come running home.

SET UP

ACTIVITY

• A whiteboard or chalkboard, overhead, PowerPoint, or something on which you can make a list while the students are answering your questions

• Markers, chalk, or overhead pen

MOVIES

- *Beauty and the Beast* (Disney)
- *Return to Me*

SONGS

- "Come Home Running," Chris Tomlin (*Not to Us*, 2002)
- "When God Ran," Phillips, Craig and Dean (*Restoration*, 1999)

MUSIC VIDEO OR SONG

- "Take You Back," Jeremy Camp (*Restored*, 2004)

SECTION 1: BACKGROUND FOR LEADERS

INSIDE-OUT SPIRITUALITY

In Ezekiel 11:14-15, we see the attitude the people left in Jerusalem have toward those who've already been carried off into Babylonian exile. Those left are convinced they're okay because they're in the land and can still worship at the temple. Now as we saw in session 4 (Ezekiel 8), these people were worshiping at the temple in the worst possible way, but they thought they were still valid as long as they were at the temple. And, clearly, in their point of view, it was the exiles who had messed up, and Yahweh had cast them out, leaving the people in Jerusalem, who were in good standing. Okay, so this is messed-up logic in light of what we've been discussing. My question is, *What perceived differences were there between the exiles and those left in Jerusalem, when they all had been committing the same sins in the sight of the LORD?*

Because those left in Jerusalem thought they were in good standing with God, they thought they had the right to take possession of the lands of those who were in Babylon. Now here's an example of some seriously bad exegesis; I mean, what Scripture were they reading? The Ten Commandments clearly talk about this business of putting other gods before God (Exodus 20:3-4). But they thought they were okay because they were worshiping at the temple site.

See, this is what happens when we get so focused on the external appearances of spirituality—we forget about the inward relationship. It's so easy to fall into the trap of thinking that if we attend church regularly, have our quiet times, or do whatever counts as a sign of "being spiritual," we're okay. It's not that those things aren't important; it's just that they aren't enough. And by themselves, they're useless. Without the dynamic and intimate, personal relationship, the outward signs are nothing. This is what God is telling the people by saying: "I have been a sanctuary for them in the countries where they have gone" (Ezekiel 11:16). The language of sanctuary for these people was reserved for the physical location of their temple. Here God is saying that he himself will be what they thought the temple actually was, when in fact, the temple was merely a representation of the sanctuary of the relationship with God.

The relationship Yahweh desires with the exiles requires a spirituality that has nothing to do with the outward signs, trappings, or traditional housings we typically associate with spirituality. This is a relationship separate from the temple, which the Israelites are used to being the focal point for their relationship with God. The temple was the outward sign that God was with them. But, since it had been turned into a sort of automatic guarantee in their minds that God was with them so long as they were going there, God is changing things up in order to turn their attention back to their relationship with God in this chapter.

PREEMPTIVE GRACE

As we saw in session 4, the Israelites had fallen away from God within one generation of major reforms. And even now, those in exile aren't listening to what the prophet Ezekiel has to say. Even worse, the rest of the book will provide no indication that they listen to anything Ezekiel says to them. And yet here in this passage, we find God's grace at work before Israel even recognizes she needs to respond when God says, "I will gather you from the nations and bring you back from the countries where you have been scattered, and I will give you back the land of Israel again" (verse 17). God makes a plan to redeem Israel way before she recognizes her need for it, just as God planned and made a way to redeem you and me long before we were even born and definitely before we were capable of recognizing our need for it. Here we see God's heart and agenda in history—to bring people back into relationship with him, to give people a second chance at prospering even though they don't deserve it.

DIVINE REDEMPTION

The book of Ruth is an important and memorable example of how the Old Testament concept of a kinsman-redeemer functioned. When a man died, his closest kin would buy his land, and, if he weren't already married, or often even if he were married, he would marry his relative's widow and raise children who would bear the dead man's name. That way, the man's property stayed in the family, his family was provided for, and his line wasn't lost among his clan. This is how God is planning to function by saying he will give them back the land of Israel (verse 17). The land was theirs, but they lost it through turning away from God and breaking the covenant with him. So God here acts as a "kinsman-redeemer" in giving the land back to Israel.

TRANSFORMATION AND RESTORATION

In order to be in a place where God could do all this—to really understand all that had happened and to really respond and relate to God—Israel needed to sign up for a heart transplant. The biggest problem with the Israelites is that their hearts had become calloused and unresponsive toward God. Their hearts were hearts of stone (verse 19). God's plans call for new hearts. Notice, this transplant isn't something the Israelites can do themselves; it's clearly God who takes out their hearts of stone and replaces them with hearts of flesh. We can never reform ourselves to a place where we can truly relate to God. He has to give us that ability. We have the choice, however, of whether or not to sign up for this heart transplant by responding to his offer of grace.

SECTION 2: MAKING IT LIVE FOR YOUR STUDENTS

INTRODUCTION: DEFINING A "GOOD" CHRISTIAN

Ask your students: *What makes someone a "good" Christian?* Write their responses where they can see them. After you've collected perhaps two dozen answers or they stop talking, whichever comes first, ask them to place their responses into two categories: "inside" and "outside." For example, going to church would be an outside characteristic, whereas faith would be an inside one. Granted, someone's faith can cause him to do many things that are external and visible, including going to church—but just because someone goes to church doesn't mean he has faith.

Chances are, you'll have a lot more "external" things than internal things. Ask: *What could be some of the motivations for these "external" things?* Your students might come up with answers such as appearance, family ties, and wanting to make friends and meet people, along with wanting to grow closer to God, be obedient to him, learn more about him, and so forth. External expressions of faith are certainly important, but the outside has to come from the inside. The other way around doesn't work.

Read Ezekiel 11:14-15 out loud to your students.

• *What are the people left in Jerusalem saying about the people who were carried off to exile?* The people in Jerusalem think it's only the people in exile who sinned.

• *What do you think might be their reasoning for why they're okay?* They think that since they're still worshiping at the temple, they're okay with God.

• *How were they worshiping in the temple, though?* Get someone to summarize some of the things the people were doing, discussed in session 4.

• Explain: *So, if the worship at the temple wasn't the kind of worship that was glorifying to God and he wasn't happy about it, then clearly the people left in Jerusalem were just as bad as the people who'd been carried off into exile. They think they're all good because they're worshiping at the temple and that's all that counts.*

• *We just reviewed how the people were worshiping idols in the temple. What did this say about the people's hearts?* Their hearts weren't focused on God, and he viewed their actions as adultery.

• *So, what does God care about?* He's interested in the people's hearts, not just in what they do on the outside.

MOVIE CLIP: *BEAUTY AND THE BEAST*—INSIDE OUT

Play clip 1.
START [00:07:53] STOP [00:08:51]

• *Why doesn't Belle want to pay attention to Gaston?*

• *For those of you who've seen this movie before, what is Belle's reaction when she first meets the Beast?*

Play clip 2. START [00:54:05] STOP [00:56:00]

• *In the second clip, what has changed in Belle's opinion of the Beast?*

• *Compare Belle's new reaction to the Beast with her reaction to Gaston at the beginning of the film...*

• *Based on that, what could we say matters most to Belle?* She's interested in what's inside.

• Explain: *The Beast's transformation (optional third scene START [01:21:15] STOP [01:25:20]) also is a good example of how someone's outside life will eventually mirror the inside life. And that can actually affect appearance in real life, too.*

• *Have you ever known someone who you thought was an attractive person until you got to know him or her?*

• *Or how about someone who wasn't terribly attractive physically, but once you discovered what a beautiful person he or she was, you started seeing that person as more attractive physically?*

• Summarize: *The Beast was cursed because of his beastly behavior to a woman in need. Through that curse, he learned his lesson, and through Belle's love, his good side came out and eventually caused his transformation into the handsome prince. This is what God wants to do for us: change us on the inside so the outside will reflect his work in us.*

PROVIDING GRACE

Pick several volunteers, and have them each read a verse of Ezekiel 11:16-21.

• *Describe how well the people of Israel have been listening to God speaking through Ezekiel at this point in our study.*

• *So even though Israel hasn't listened and hasn't responded to what God has been saying, what is God planning to do in the passage we just read?* Here in this passage, we find God's grace at work before Israel even recognizes that she needs to respond when God says, "I will gather you from the nations and bring you back from the countries where you have been scattered, and I will give you back the land of Israel again" (verse 17).

• Summarize: *God makes a plan to redeem Israel way before she recognizes her need for it, just as God planned and made a way to redeem you and me long before we were even born and definitely before we were capable of recognizing our need for it. Here we see God's heart and agenda in history—to bring people back into relationship with him, to give people a second chance at prospering even though they don't deserve it.*

MOVIE CLIP: *RETURN TO ME*—HEART TRANSPLANT

The premise of the movie is that Grace gets Bob's wife's heart after she dies in a car accident, and the heart stays faithful to Bob and causes Grace to fall in love with him. Now, granted, the literal heart in our chest that beats and keeps us alive isn't the center of love and can't make the decision to remain faithful, but the idea that the heart transplant is what allows her to fall in love with this man is a useful illustration of what God wants to do for Israel.

Play clip 1. START [00:08:05] STOP [00:09:36] (Grace in the hospital)

• Explain: *Grace would have died without a heart transplant. Now, does anyone know how you get a new heart? Other than the surgery aspect...* You have to be on a waiting list until the right heart comes along.

• *So Grace had to have been on a list to get a heart. She wasn't required to put herself on the list. She could have tried to pretend that everything was fine until she ended up in the hospital where we see her in this first clip. But it takes a long time to get a heart transplant, and if she had waited until she was in the hospital to get one, she would have died before getting one.*

• *Obviously, it would have been stupid for her not to sign up for a heart transplant. What was Grace admitting by signing up for a heart transplant?* She was acknowledging that she was dying and in need of some major help; she couldn't do for herself.

• *In the passage we just read, what do you think Israel's problem was?* The biggest problem with the Israelites is that their hearts had become calloused and unresponsive toward God. Their hearts were hearts of stone (verse 19). In God's plan, a heart transplant is the first order of business.

• *In order to be in a place where God could do all of this—to really understand all that had happened and to really respond and relate to God—Israel needed to sign up for a heart transplant.*

- *Now, in verse 19, who is doing the action?* This heart transplant isn't something the Israelites can do themselves; it's clearly God who takes out their hearts of stone and replaces them with hearts of flesh.

- Explain: *We can never reform ourselves to a place where we can truly relate to God. He has to give us that ability. We have the choice, however, of whether or not to sign up for this heart transplant by responding to his offer of grace.*

- Connect: *Just like Grace signs up for a heart transplant in the movie, we also need to sign up for our "heart transplant" from God. We need major help to turn our lives around—it's not something we can do for ourselves.*

- *What do you think signing up for a heart transplant from God looks like? What sorts of changes would he make?*

- Summarize: *To "sign up" for a heart transplant from God means acknowledging that if we continue in sin, it will kill us. And even if we've already turned our lives over to God and made a commitment to him, if we continue to let some sort of sin go unaddressed in our lives, it will rob us of living a complete life in God.*

Play clip 2. START [00:32:11] STOP [00:33:01]
Play clip 3. START [00:43:43] STOP [00:48:21] (Restaurant scene)

- *What is the significance of the first clip?* This clip is showing that Grace's heart does something when Bob walks by her. She doesn't know what it is or why it happens.

- *What happens in the second clip?* Grace's new heart gives her the ability to respond to Bob. They both have the impression they already know each other, and that feeling of familiarity ends up jump-starting a relationship.

- Explain: *She ends up falling in love with him and getting to start a life with him that she never would have had if she didn't get a transplant. When God gives us a new heart, we are then able to respond to him, and that gives us the opportunity to start a new life with him we would never be able to start on our own. Just as Grace had to sign up for a heart transplant, but someone else had to do the surgery on her, we have to let God do the surgery on us.*

- *Imagine the mess we'd make if we tried to do surgery on ourselves…I mean, think about it. You'd probably faint after you made the first incision and then bleed to death. Right? I mean, it's safe to say that self-surgery isn't the smartest thing in the world to do…*

There's a section in *The Voyage of the Dawn Treader* from the Chronicles of Narnia that beautifully illustrates what it's like when we try to get out of the mess we've gotten ourselves into without God's help. I'm going to give you a synopsis of the story, but I recommend reading Lewis' version and then paraphrasing it yourself to your students with quotations where you think they'll be helpful.

In chapter 6 of The Voyage of the Dawn Treader, *"The Adventures of Eustace," Lewis tells us about Eustace going into a dragon's lair and coveting the dragon's gold. Eustace puts on a bracelet and then falls asleep. In the morning, he awakes to find out that he is, in fact, a dragon. Now, if you read the beginning of the book until this point, you will discover that Eustace has been a pain (at best!) to all those aboard the* Dawn Treader *with him, so his transformation into a dragon represents his condition on the inside all along. Well, he ends up back at camp where the rest of the people are, and they discover that the dragon is, in fact, Eustace. When he had become a dragon, his arm (paw?) swelled up, and now the bracelet he had put on is causing him constant pain. When he joins the others, they try to help his hurting arm. Their kindness to him despite his behavior throughout the story and the fact that he's now a dragon makes him realize how terrible he'd been all along.*

In chapter 7, "How the Adventure Ended," Lewis tells us how Eustace meets Aslan, the king, and Aslan leads him to a well that's feeding a bath. Eustace is sure that if he can get in the water, then it will soothe the pain from the bracelet. Aslan stops him and tells him he has to undress first. Eustace tries to get out of his scaly dragon skin by scratching around on the ground, and sure enough, off comes a layer. But when he looks at his reflection in the water, he realizes he has another layer on. So he scratches around again to remove another layer and then another, but it does no good. Aslan then says, "You will have to let me undress you."[10] Eustace is afraid of the lion's claws, but he's so desperate that he's willing to try anything. He lies down on his back, and Aslan starts peeling away the skin. Eustace later tells Edmund,

> *"The very first tear he made was so deep that I thought it had gone right into my heart. And when he began pulling the skin off, it hurt worse than anything I've ever felt. The only thing that made me able to bear it was just the pleasure of feeling the stuff peel off. You know—if you've ever picked a scab off a sore place. It hurts like billy-oh but it* is *fun to see it coming away."*

> *"I know exactly what you mean," said Edmund.*

> *"Well he peeled the beastly stuff right off—just as I thought I'd done it myself the other three times, only they hadn't hurt—and there it was, lying on the grass: only ever so much thicker, and darker, and more knobbly-looking than the others had been. And there was I as smooth and soft as a peeled switch and smaller than I had been. Then he caught hold of me—I didn't like that much for I was very tender underneath now that I'd no skin on—and threw me into the water. It smarted like anything but only for a moment. After that, it became perfectly delicious and as soon as I started swimming and splashing I found that all the pain had gone from my arm. And then I saw why. I'd turned into a boy again."[11]*

After this, Eustace tells Edmond that Aslan dressed him in new clothes. This excerpt is really a cool idea of what it's like to turn your life over to God, have him baptize you and dress you in the robes of his righteousness, and then have you go back to the world still marveling at what happened and trying to figure out your change of heart.

[10] Lewis, *The Chronicles of Narnia*, 474.
[11] Ibid., 474-75.

COME HOME RUNNING

Conclude: *The moral of the story for us, then, is that God is in a place where we can find him, and he's waiting for us to sign up for a heart transplant so he can fix us. It doesn't matter how far we've gone, what we've done, or how bad of shape we're in—he's waiting and hoping for us to turn around and come to him just as we are. For we can't fix ourselves; only God can do that. We simply have to respond and offer up our mess—our broken lives—to him and let him go about restoring what was lost, healing what was broken, bringing life where there was death. This God of ours is passionate about his relationship with us; and right now, regardless of how messed up we think our lives are, God, in his grace, has already planned how to restore us and make us whole again.*

CLOSING

Pass out the journaling exercise, **Signing Up for a Heart Transplant**. Encourage your students to write a prayer, talking to God about where they are and what they think about this whole heart-transplant idea. Play "When God Ran" by Phillips, Craig, and Dean (*Restoration*, 1998) and "Take You Back" by Jeremy Camp (*Restored*, 2004) while the students journal. If you have PowerPoint capability, then create a presentation with the lyrics and perhaps nature pictures. (If you don't have pictures for worship presentations, check out www.sxc.hu, a free stock-photography site where you can download all sorts of creative photos to use as backgrounds. Some of them require permission from the artist, but most of them don't. Check restrictions at the bottom of the photo.) Having the PowerPoint (or MediaShout) images playing along with the song creates an atmosphere to "surround" the students with the lyrics in a sense. Or you could play the music video of "Take You Back."

For a closing song, singing "Come Home Running" by Chris Tomlin (*Not to Us*, 2002) would be appropriate, or you could use this song for the journaling time if you prefer. (You can get these songs or the video from iTunes for $0.99/song or $1.99/video.)

JOURNALING: SIGNING UP FOR A HEART TRANSPLANT

In the movie clips we watched from Return to Me, Grace had to sign up for a heart transplant. Now, it's obvious in the film that she needed one desperately, but just as desperately as she needed a physical heart transplant, we need a spiritual heart transplant.

What do you think about this idea of a spiritual heart transplant?

Have you ever asked God to give you his heart toward people or situations in your life? Would you be willing to?

Write a prayer talking to God about where you are and what you think about this whole heart-transplant idea…

ARE THERE IDOLS IN YOUR HEART?

SESSION 6: EZEKIEL 14:1-5; 1 CORINTHIANS 6:19-20

OVERVIEW

Ezekiel 14 gives a fantastic description of idols in the temple. When we remember that our bodies are temples of the Holy Spirit (1 Corinthians 6:19-20), this passage offers a wonderful picture of the seriousness of erecting idols in our own lives. This parallel is nicely established between the images of idols in the temple in Ezekiel 8 and the consequences of idols in our hearts in Ezekiel 14.

SET UP

MOVIE

• *Star Wars - Episode III, Revenge of the Sith*

SONGS

• "Empty Me," Jeremy Camp (*Carried Me*, 2004)
• "Deliver Me," David Crowder Band (*Illuminate*, 2003)

SECTION 1: BACKGROUND FOR LEADERS

GOD IS NOT A GENIE

The leaders of Israel are hoping for a word from God that will tell them when this horrible exile is to end, and they can return to their homes. Essentially, they're coming to God and asking for an out from the consequences of their sin when they won't even recognize that they're in sin. They are unrepentant, still longing for the idolatrous ways they practiced in Israel, and yet they want God to get them out of exile. Notice, too, that they go to Ezekiel the prophet and try to get a word from God in Ezekiel 14. They had already been given abundant words from God, complete with sign acts to form visual images of precisely what was going to happen.

In Ezekiel 8 (session 4), Ezekiel has a vision of all the abominations going on in what is supposed to be the temple of the LORD. At the end of Ezekiel 8, we see him relate that vision to the elders of Judah who were gathered at his house—probably for the exact same reason these elders of Israel were gathered at his house the day we're looking at now. And you know people are going to talk. Most likely, the story of Ezekiel's vision would have gotten around the community of exiles. I mean, Ezekiel was one of their chief sources of entertainment. And in Ezekiel 33:30-33, God clearly tells Ezekiel that the people are all talking about him and what he says, but they treat him as an entertainer—one who tells stories and sings songs for the amusement of the people.

So despite the fact that it should have been very clear to these elders who show up at Ezekiel's house this day that Yahweh has a beef with them because of their idol worship, they want to treat Ezekiel like he's some medium who can manipulate the deity into giving them the answer they want. This is how far gone they are. They're treating the God of Israel like any other run-of-the-mill deity who could be cajoled or appeased into acting the way the questioner desired. But the God of Israel—your God and my God—is no run-of-the-mill deity, and he most certainly is not a genie somehow compelled to grant your wish.

CONFUSING THE GIFT WITH THE GIVER

How could these elders have gotten so far in their thinking that they would treat God so? Part of the problem—perhaps a big part—was the way they viewed their land. See, the land of Israel was a gift from God to his people. It's the land promised to Abraham in Genesis, and it's the land God brought his people back to after he rescued them from Egypt. Remember that the people of Israel were in Egypt for entirely different reasons from why they're now in Babylon. Egypt was actually a gift from God in the days of Joseph. It was how God provided for his people when a famine was in the land. But times changed, a new Pharaoh got into power, and the Israelites were enslaved. So God went down and rescued them. It was such a dramatic event in Israel's history that one of the ways they indicated which God was theirs was by calling him "the God who brought us up out of Egypt."

But now these people are in Babylon because they had turned away from God and started worshiping idols. God gave them up to their own devices and let them taste the consequences of their sin (see Romans 1:22-25 and additional information at the end of the Background for Leaders section), one, because God won't protect and put his seal of approval on sin, and two, because he was hoping the exile would get their attention and bring them back into relationship with him. But here they are, thinking God's primary objective is to get them back into the land, because that would show the other nations he was more powerful than the other gods. See, like we've discussed a couple of times before, the people had a very strong notion that Yahweh was tied to the land of Israel, and as long as they were in Yahweh's land, they were under his protection. And they thought they could do whatever they wanted because Yahweh would still act on their behalf against opposing nations. This misguided notion came from their dabbling in syncretism, meaning they were trying to practice paganism along with the worship of God. And so they mapped onto God these ideas that neighboring nations had about their deities.

They thought that after God brought them out of Egypt, and they arrived in the land, they were now safe and secure. Worse yet, they became so satiated in their security they forgot just how much they needed God and how exactly they had gotten to where they were anyway. Ultimately, this resulted in turning the land itself into an idol. See, when someone's focus gets shifted from the Giver to the gift, the gift itself can become an idol. God gave the land of Israel to the people so they would have a safe place to be in relationship with him. He didn't care about the land. The land was a metaphor; God was the reality (Psalm 61:1-2). And God cares about the people's hearts, which he clearly says in this passage in Ezekiel 14. In verse 4, the LORD refuses to answer their questions, instead telling them that when an idolatrous person comes before him and wants an answer, God only deals with that person according to his or her idolatry. Then verse 5, the pivotal verse for this section, reveals the LORD's heart in this matter. He says, "I will do this to recapture the hearts of the people of Israel, who have all deserted me for their idols." To recapture their hearts—this is the goal of this God who is passionately and irrevocably in love with his people despite their wandering hearts and idolatrous ways. God's not writing them off and going to look for a new relationship somewhere else; God continues to pursue them to recapture their hearts.

ADDITIONAL INFORMATION

Immediately following our passage, we have an incredibly difficult verse. It's not part of the session, but I want to touch on it briefly in case any of your kids brings it up. Ezekiel 14:9 says, "And if the prophet is enticed to utter a prophecy, I the LORD have enticed that prophet, and I will stretch out my hand against him and destroy him from among my people Israel." On the surface it looks like God's saying he's going to deceive prophets and then destroy them for uttering a false message. However, in verse 8, God says that if the people who have turned away from him and are worshiping idols go to a prophet in an unrepentant state and try to get a word from the LORD, he won't answer them. Thus, that prophet will have no prophecy to give, and if he's truly following God, that prophet will know that God won't respond to people who come to him like that. Yet there remains the temptation within the prophet to give an answer. After all, that's what prophets do—they give words from God. They often answer questions people have for God by giving them a word from God. But if the people have no relationship with God, going to a prophet will only hurt them, not help them. And the test for the prophet shows if he will be faithful to the LORD and remain silent.

In 1 Kings 22, we have an example of this sort of thing happening. Here Ahab, the king of Israel, wants to go to war, and he asks Jehoshaphat, king of Judah, to go join with him. Jehoshaphat agrees, but only if they first seek the counsel of the LORD. But what does Ahab do? Ahab calls together no fewer than 400 prophets who aren't prophets of the LORD and asks them what he should do. Their response is a unanimous, "Go for it!" Jehoshaphat recognizes that these aren't prophets of the LORD and asks, "Is there not a prophet of the LORD here whom we can inquire of?" (1 Kings 22:7).

Ahab reluctantly calls Micaiah, whom he doesn't like because Micaiah never says anything good about him. The messenger he sends tells Micaiah that these other prophets are predicting success and advises him to do the same. (You know, these Old Testament kings, they had habits of lopping people's heads off who ticked them off.) Micaiah responds, "As surely as the LORD lives, I can tell him only what the LORD tells me" (1 Kings 22:14). So, here we have a case of an idolatrous king who has sent for a prophet of the LORD and is looking for God's help when his heart is far away from God, just like the situation in Ezekiel 14. To Ahab's surprise, Micaiah tells him, "Attack and be victorious for the LORD will give it into the king's hand" (1 Kings 22:15). Of course, I would want to know what the LORD was giving and who the king was, and Ahab himself doubts the prophecy. So Micaiah gives him some unparalleled insight into the mind of God. He tells him he saw all of Israel scattered like sheep without a shepherd, which ticks Ahab off. Then Micaiah proceeds to tell Ahab that God wanted to kill him, so he allowed a spirit to go put a false word in all the other prophets' mouths so Ahab would be enticed into battle and killed. (Now, if that's not spelling it out, I don't know what is.) But does Ahab listen? Of course not. He goes into battle, albeit in disguise, and dies. The battle is lost, and Israel is without a king, just as Micaiah said.

Perhaps Romans 1 will shed even more light on this concept. Verses 22-25 talk about people exchanging "the glory of the immortal God for images made to look like mortal man and birds and animals and reptiles." Because of this, "God gave them over in the sinful desires of their hearts to sexual impurity for the degrading of their bodies with one another." Ultimately, what these people had done, and what the people in Ezekiel's day had done, was "exchanged the truth of God for a lie, and worshiped and served created things rather than the Creator." So God gave them up to the results of their own idolatry. And this is what he's doing with these people— giving them up and refusing to answer their presumptuous questions.

SECTION 2: MAKING IT LIVE FOR YOUR STUDENTS

INTRODUCTION

MOVIE CLIP: *STAR WARS - EPISODE III, REVENGE OF THE SITH*

In this clip, we see Anakin Skywalker make his final, irreversible steps to becoming Darth Vader. How does he get there?

Play the clip. START [01:42:42] STOP [01:47:30]

• *What were some of the steps that led Anakin to the Sith lord?*

• *What was his motivation for trying to get more power?* Probably some will answer that it was his love for Padme. If that happens, ask how he treated Padme at the end of the film and if that showed his love for her. Then ask what else was motivating him.

• *What did Anakin ultimately want?* Ultimately, because Anakin had such a high view of his own power, he thought his dreams were prophetic. He kept dreaming that Padme, his wife, would die during childbirth, and he was sure he could find a way to keep that from happening.

• *What was Anakin's view of himself?* Because of this high view of his own power, the emperor could seduce Anakin into shifting to the dark side by promising he could manipulate the Force to such an extent that he could bring people back to life.

• *What were Anakin's real priorities when it gets down to the end?* Ultimately, the power itself became his goal, as you can see by his treatment of Padme when he thinks she led Obi-Wan to him.

• Explain: *As a result, Anakin ends up fulfilling his own "prophetic" dream in a way. Padme doesn't die because of complications in childbirth (note that in the scene before the babies are born, the doctors say everything is normal, but for reasons they can't explain, they're losing her); rather, she dies of a broken heart because of Anakin's actions. This particular scene shows just how twisted Anakin's thinking has become, as he accuses Obi-Wan of turning Padme against him, and Obi-Wan tells him Anakin has done that himself.*

• Summarize: *Anakin's lust for power ended up tripping him up big time. And the thing he had feared the most—losing Padme—happened as a result of what he did. Even though people were trying to help him all along, he kept going further and further to the dark side, until he faced consequences that couldn't be undone. Padme dies, and he loses both legs and an arm and is so badly burned he has to live in a suit that helps him breathe.*

Okay, so that's depressing. But remember, even in the movie series, we see redemption, because when Anakin's son Luke, then grown, confronts him, Anakin ends up turning again to the good side and kills the emperor, giving up his life for his son. So in the end, we see Anakin with Obi-Wan and Yoda in whatever afterlife they supposedly had. If we can take from the Star Wars *movies that when we prioritize the wrong stuff in our lives, it leads to consequences that might not be reversible, but redemption is available, how much more can we see this theme in our God working in history?*

DIGGING IN: GETTING IN OUR OWN WAY

Say: *Remember when we talked about the idols the Israelites had set up in the temple? Let's list some of the things God was upset about in that session...* If they don't remember, have them open to Ezekiel 8 and quickly list the things the Israelites had done.

Have your students flip over to chapter 14. Pick two people to alternate reading verses 1-5 aloud.

• Say: *Here in chapter 14, we find out more about what's on God's heart regarding idols. For now it's not just the idols in the temple that God is concerned about, but that the idols in the physical temple represent something far more deadly—idols in the hearts of the people.*

• *If idols are things we put before or in the place of God, what are some examples of idols we set up in our hearts, often without even thinking about it?*

• Say: *Setting up idols in their hearts created lots of commitments that led the people away from God. God says: "When any Israelite sets up idols in his heart" that person "puts a wicked stumbling block before his face" (verse 4).*

• Ask: *What do you suppose God is talking about when he says "a wicked stumbling block"?* If they're unsure how to answer this question, try asking, "What do you think the concept of a 'stumbling block' sounds like?" Stumbling blocks are things that trip people up in their lives.

• *If it's safe to say the things that trip us up are a result of things we've prioritized before God, then whose fault is it when we make mistakes? Has God let us down?* The idea is if we make commitments that lead us away from God, we are setting ourselves up for a fall.

• Summarize: *It's not that God has let us down—just as he didn't let the Israelites down—rather, our behavior creates a mess. And after we've created this mess, God won't stop the consequences of our actions.*

RECAPTURING HEARTS

We've seen this far in the book of Ezekiel that God is interested in a relationship with us. God has tried and tried to get his people's attention, and we've seen how their repeated and unrepentant unfaithfulness to him has broken his heart. But even in the consequences of their (and our) actions, God is working to call them back to him.

• *What is the key line in this week's passage* (Ezekiel 14:1-5) *that tells us what God wants to do for his people?* God's goal is to "recapture the hearts of the people of Israel, who have all deserted me for their idols."

• *When a person talks about "capturing" someone's heart, what kind of language is that?* This is the language of courtship and romance, which shows the kind of love God has for us, his people.

GOD IS NOT A GENIE

God's efforts to recapture the hearts of his people are just one more piece of evidence, showing us just how much he loves us and how much he wants a real relationship with us.

• *How often do we go to God and give him a to-do list when we pray?* If your students get really quiet and don't want to really "fess up" on this one, you might say that this is a tendency we all fall into a lot and then go to the next question.

• *If the bulk of our prayers have to do with presenting God with a list of requests, how are we treating God?*

• Summarize: *This is treating God like a genie who will grant our wishes if we rub him the right way.*

• *With that in mind, what do you think the leaders of Israel are looking for when they come to Ezekiel?* They're looking for a word from God.

• *Have they had other opportunities to hear what God was saying? When?* Students should list some of the things discussed in past sessions regarding Ezekiel's messages to the people.

GOD IS THE GIFT; EVERYTHING ELSE IS A BONUS

How could these elders have gotten so far in their thinking that they would treat God like this? Part of the problem—perhaps a big part—was the way they viewed their land.

• *Does anyone know where the land of Israel came from?* The land of Israel was a gift from God to his people.

• Explain: *The land of Israel was promised to Abraham in Genesis, and it's the land that God brought his people back to after he rescued them from Egypt. Remember, the people of Israel were in Egypt for entirely different reasons from why they're now in Babylon. Egypt was actually a gift from God in the days of Joseph. It was how God provided for his people when a famine was in the land. But times changed, a new Pharaoh came into power, and the Israelites were enslaved. So God went down and rescued them. It was such a dramatic event in Israel's history that one of the ways they referred to God was as "the God who brought us up out of Egypt."*

But now the people are in Babylon because they have turned away from God and started worshiping idols.

• *Why do you think God allowed Israel to be carried off to Babylon?* God allowed this to happen because he won't protect and put his seal of approval on sin, and because he was hoping exile would get their attention and bring them back into relationship with him.

• *What would other nations have thought about God if he protected them no matter what they did?*

• Summarize: *The other nations wouldn't have gotten a good picture of what kind of God our God is if he just protected people no matter what they did. God's goal is relationships.*

• Explain: *The people here are thinking that God's primary objective is to get them back into the land, because that would show the surrounding nations he was more powerful than their gods. The Israelites thought God would be more interested in protecting his reputation by not letting his people get defeated, but as we've seen, God is interested in relationships with people.*

• *They thought that after God brought them out of Egypt, and they arrived in the land, they were now safe and secure. Worse yet, they became so satisfied in their security they forgot how much they needed God and how they had gotten to this place of safety.*

• *So, if the people ended up putting the land and the security it gave them in front of their relationship with God, what does that make the land in God's view?* Ultimately, the land itself was turned into an idol.

• Explain: *When the focus gets shifted from the Giver onto the gift, then the gift itself can become an idol. God gave the land of Israel to the people so they would have a safe place to be in relationship with him. God didn't care about the land—he cared about the relationship with his people.*

• Read: *"I will do this to recapture the hearts of the people of Israel, who have all deserted me for their idols"* (verse 5).

• Ask: *This is chapter 14 of the book of Ezekiel. How much progress has Ezekiel made? Has God given up? What does that tell us about God?* He's not giving up easily, and he won't give up easily on us, either.

WHAT'S IT ALL MEAN?

Conclude: *The point is that it simply will not do to turn away from God, commit to idols in our hearts, and then go running to God after we've tripped over the stumbling blocks we've put in our own paths because of our rebellion, and then try to get God to get us out of our predicament without repenting! God is in the business of straightening up lives and restoring things that are lost and broken and seemingly without hope. But his one and only requirement for beginning to do this in our lives is that we come to him, recognizing we are hopelessly lost in our sins and unable to free ourselves from the consequences, and repent for what we've done. By doing that we throw ourselves into the best possible situation, and that is wholly and completely at God's mercy. And with mercy and grace, he won't give us what our sins deserve* (Psalm 103:10) *but will grant us everlasting life through Jesus Christ our* LORD.

CLOSING

Pass out the journaling exercise, **Getting Out of Our Own Way**. Encourage your students to write a prayer talking to God about where they are and what they think about recognizing that God can straighten up and restore broken lives, but only when those lives are given to him. Play "Empty Me" by Jeremy Camp (*Carried Me*, 2004) while the students journal. If you have PowerPoint capability, then create a presentation with the lyrics and perhaps nature pictures. (If you don't have pictures for worship presentations, check out www.sxc.hu, a free stock-photography site where you can download all sorts of creative photos to use as backgrounds. Some of them require permission from the artist, but most of them don't. Check restrictions at the bottom of the photo.) Having the PowerPoint (or MediaShout) images playing along with the song creates an atmosphere to "surround" the students with the lyrics in a sense.

For a closing song, singing "Deliver Me" by the David Crowder Band (*Illuminate*, 2003) would be appropriate. (You can get these songs from iTunes for $0.99 each.)

JOURNALING: GETTING OUT OF OUR OWN WAY

Where in your life do you have commitments that might lead you away from God?

What kind of stumbling blocks have they caused? Could they cause?

What do you know you need God's help with in your life right now?

Talk to God about what you need him to empty you of or deliver you from…

YOU SHOULD BE DEAD

SESSION 7: EZEKIEL 18 (ESPECIALLY VERSES 30-32); JOHN 3:16; ROMANS 8:28

OVERVIEW

"The soul who sins will die" reads the heading for this chapter in the New International Version. According to Ezekiel 18, if you've sinned, you should be dead. But God in his love provides a way out through repentance. "For God so loved the world…" What are you going to do with God's radical love?

SET UP

PREPARE

• Practice reading Ezekiel 18 (see Introduction).

MOVIE

• *Signs*

SECTION 1: BACKGROUND FOR LEADERS

GOD IS INTERESTED IN THE HEART OF THE INDIVIDUAL

Ezekiel 18 pulls together ideas from chapters 3, 11, 14, and 33 that we've looked at in sessions 2, 5, and 6. Here we find reiterated in no uncertain terms that God is interested in the heart of the individual as the means to transform the entire community. If a whole nation is to be saved, it must happen one person at a time.

The structure of this chapter is Ezekiel refuting three popular misconceptions about the nature of God. The first is found in verse 2, which I believe the New Living Translation renders most accurately: "The parents have eaten sour grapes, but their children's mouths pucker at the taste." This notion of puckering is what the NIV (and other translations) implies when it says, "the children's teeth are set on edge." What it reflects is a sort of cosmic determinism whereby the children are punished for their parents' sins. This seems to be a prevailing concept among nations of that day, and we find the same proverb verbatim in Jeremiah 31:29. Jeremiah was prophesying at roughly the same time as Ezekiel, but Jeremiah was back in Jerusalem prophesying to the people who had not yet been exiled. Thus we see that God is working in many spheres to turn the hearts of the people back to himself.

What this repeated proverb reveals is that the people with whom Ezekiel dialogues in this chapter believe they—the exiles—are, in fact, innocent; they're paying for sins their parents committed. Now that we've read about the idolatry in Ezekiel 8 and 14 (sessions 4 and 6), it's really impossible for us to believe these people are innocent. Yet this is their mindset, even after everything Ezekiel has done at God's prompting to try to tell them about their sins, so they could repent, come back to God, and find new life, new hope, and a future that God has planned for them (Jeremiah 29:11).

REFUTING COSMIC DETERMINISM

Ezekiel goes about refuting this concept of cosmic determinism (i.e., because parents had sinned, their children would suffer; life was just that way, and no one can do anything about it). In 18:3-18, Ezekiel presents the people with the true reality about God. God starts out by instructing the people to never repeat this false proverb again. Then God goes on to affirm in verse 4 that each person's life is in his hands, and only the person who sins will be judged for it: "The soul who sins is the one who will die."

Then come three hypothetical case studies to represent three generations of men. The first, found in verses 5-9, tells of the righteous grandfather. The list in this passage probably represents commonly accepted marks of righteousness. After this list, verse 9 affirms that this man "follows my decrees and faithfully keeps my laws. That man is righteous; he will surely live…" By contrast we find essentially the same list, but in the negative, in verses 10-13. Here's the case of the wicked son who rebels against God and the way his father lived and does everything opposite of what is righteous. The end of verse 13 exclaims that such a man will certainly not live.

Then we find the third case in verses 14-18, which is the case of the righteous grandson. The grandson looks at how his father lived and decides to follow the LORD, and in that, he ends up imitating his grandfather as well. In verse 17, we find another affirmation that the grandson will live and not be punished in any way for the sins of his father.

All three cases have nearly the same list and outline three key areas in which people need to be obedient. Those three areas are: (1) God's sovereignty, (2) sexuality, and (3) economics (treating people fairly).[12] God's purpose for including these case studies is to spell out for the people of Israel that (1) he doesn't judge people based on past generations, and thus (2) they're in exile as a result of their own collective sins as a nation.

A NEW VISION OF GOD

"This is what Ezekiel's audience needs to deliver them from their bondage of depression and despair—a new vision of God, a God who is on the side of blessing and life, not on the side of the curse and death."[13] And I think we, too, need a new vision of God. Ours is not a God who makes everything happen for a reason so we can learn a lesson. Despite this popular sentiment, that is actually an Islamic view of God. In Islam, Allah is the originator of everything—good and bad alike—and the bad things he sends to you are to test you to see if you'll still follow him. Our God, by contrast, is working in all things for the good of those who love him and are called according to his purpose (Romans 8:28). There's a world of difference between causing bad things to happen and working in bad things to redeem the situation and use it for the good of the person. Our God says in Jeremiah 9:24, "but let those who boast boast in this, that they understand and know me, that I am the LORD; I act with steadfast love, justice, and righteousness in the earth, for *in these things I delight*, says the LORD" (NRSV, emphasis added). He *delights* in unfailing, or steadfast, love, justice, and righteousness. These are the things he employs for the good of his people. He will never fail us in his love. He will always be just, and he will always do what is right. Period.

After the lengthy explanations and repetitions of what qualifies someone for judgment, God says at the end of this chapter that he will judge the house of Israel, each one of them, according to what they've done and then pleads with them to "Repent! Turn away from all your offenses; then sin will not be your downfall" (Ezekiel 18:30). Why does God urge repentance? So sin will not be our downfall. Sin will kill us (Romans 6:23), and that's the last thing God wants to happen to the people he loves, who, by the way, are the whole world, as that famous verse John 3:16 clearly states: "For God so loved the world…" John Stott said it best about what God did to save us from our sin: "God himself gave himself to save us from himself."[14] Instead of merely giv-

---

[12] Brueggeman, *An Introduction to the Old Testament*, 207.
[13] Block, *The Book of Ezekiel: Chapters 1-24*, 583.
[14] Stott, *Romans*, 115.

ing us what we deserve—death for our sins—God gave up his own life to save us from what we justly deserve. See, it's completely just to let people die for their sins. That would be fair. But God acts with steadfast and unfailing love! His love makes him go to the ultimate lengths to provide a way for us to live! He offers us a new heart and a new spirit (Ezekiel 18:31) so we will not die. "For I take no pleasure in the death of anyone, declares the Sovereign LORD. Repent and live!" (verse 32).

SECTION 2: MAKING IT LIVE FOR YOUR STUDENTS

INTRODUCTION

Ask: *Have you ever heard someone say, "Everything happens for a reason"? How about, "It must be karma"? Let's list some examples of the kinds of situations in which these statements are used…* Mention that these popular sayings are representations of messed-up views of the way God and our world work, particularly when "everything happens for a reason" is applied to God, but don't get into why until after the movie clip.

Read Ezekiel 18 to your kids. Practice this in advance so you can read through the repetitious parts as quickly as you can enunciate them. That will make the repetitions humorous to help emphasize that God was working really hard here to get the point across to an audience who didn't want to hear him.

MOVIE CLIP: *SIGNS*—MESSED-UP VIEWS OF GOD

Play the clip. START [00:41:15] STOP [00:46:03] (Chapter 10: "Fourteen Lights")

Background to the movie: In this scene, Graham is talking to his brother Merrill about the mysterious lights that have appeared over a city. Merrill is frightened by the implications and turns to Graham for comfort. Graham is a former minister (Episcopal priest, which is why he's married with kids), who gave up his ministry because he was mad at God for allowing his wife to die. (The movie doesn't show this until the end. All the way through, the film is really about Graham coming to terms with what God allowed to happen and, through a sequence of events, having his relationship with God restored.)

• *Since Graham was a minister, it would make sense to assume he believed in God at some point. Why did he stop?* Simply—or not so simply—because his wife died in a freak accident where a driver fell asleep at the wheel and crushed her in a split second while she was taking a walk.

• *Why does Graham insist that "no one is looking out for us; we are all alone"?* Graham is mad at God and thinks God isn't watching or God isn't doing anything because God didn't do what Graham wanted him to do.

• *Hmm…sounds familiar. Where in the passage we just read from Ezekiel do you see people mad at God because God isn't doing what they want?*

• *What starts Ezekiel off on his long explanation of how only the person who sins suffers the results of that sin?* The proverb in Ezekiel 18:2.

• Explain: *The people are basically saying that they're suffering for the sins the previous generation committed.* (See the Background for Leaders section.)

• *What does God think about this proverb they're quoting?* Read verses 3-4.

TWO MORE PROVERBS AND TWO MORE RADICAL VIEWS OF GOD

• Say: *So Ezekiel goes into this long account of how God works, explaining in very thorough detail as we've just seen that it's* only *the person who sins who suffers the consequences. He spends 16 long verses to get this point across, but what do the people say in response? Somebody read the first part of verse 19 again…*

• *Why would the people want to think they're being punished for the sins of the generation before them?*

• Summarize: *They would be off the hook. They wouldn't have to do anything. No repentance, no change of heart, no change of how they live life, nothing. They're just the unfortunate casualties paying the price for their parents' sins so that God's ledger books in heaven can somehow be balanced out.*

• *Now, how do you suppose this connects to some of the popular proverbs of our day that we just mentioned, like, "Everything happens for a reason," or, "It must be karma"? What do those two statements say, in effect?* They're often tied together and go with a third idea that all of our deeds sort of "balance out," and in the end, if we've done more good than bad, we'll be okay.

• Explain: *This view of having to "balance things out" treats God as a sort of disinterested deity officiating in heaven, keeping score of everyone's life, and whoever has a positive score at the end of it all wins. This ties right into the pop view of karma that's adapted from the Buddhists; they believe in a "karmic bank account" where everything you do that's good, or done with good intentions, adds to your account, while anything bad, or done with bad intentions, subtracts from it.*[15]

• *How does Ezekiel respond to this kind of statement in the verses that follow?* Ezekiel throws that out the window rapidly by reaffirming in verse 20 that "the soul who sins is the one who will die," and in case they didn't get it, he states yet again that "the son will not share the guilt of the father, nor will the father share the guilt of the son." Instead, "the righteousness of the righteous man will be credited to him, and the wickedness of the wicked man will be charged against him."

[15] This sentence is a paraphrase from a presentation by a Buddhist nun named Jue Wei from the Hsi Lai Temple in Hacienda Heights, California, for a class I was teaching on world religions at Mt. San Antonio College in Walnut, California, in the fall of 2004.

• *What is the significance of the concept that only the people who sin will suffer for their sin?*

• Summarize: *It's like saying, "Okay, Israelites, you who are in exile, you are here because of what you did in this generation. You turned away from God and worshiped idols and pulled yourselves out of God's protection. And God desperately wants you to get this concept, not so you can realize why he's zapping you, but so you can turn and live! God doesn't take pleasure in the death of the wicked; he'd rather see wicked people turn from their sin and live* (verse 23).

• *What is the people's response to this?* They say, "The way of the LORD is not just" (verse 25).

• Say: *Notice here they've made a direct accusation against Yahweh. They've shaken their fists in the face of Almighty God and said, "It's not fair! You are unjust!" This is after they've trampled on the covenant they made with God and broken his heart by pursuing other gods and practicing self-destructive behavior.*

• *Why do they continue to throw accusations at God?* They'd rather try to prove God's unjust, and they're at the mercy of an unpredictable and arbitrary God[16] than face the fact that they've messed up and have to do something about it.

• *What does God do?* Here's the really remarkable thing about this passage—God answers them. God keeps talking to them.

• *Has God changed what he's saying?* God says the same thing yet again in verses 26-29: If you're righteous, you'll live; if you're unrighteous, you'll die.

• *Describe how God is acting in this chapter...* There's nothing arbitrary or unpredictable about how God is acting. He doesn't change what he's saying, and even though the people argue, he patiently continues to try to reveal himself to them.

• Summarize: *Even after the people have accused God of being unjust, arbitrary, and vindictive, God is still talking to them. This demonstrates incredible love and grace and shows that God is not unjust, because even after they reject everything God's done to try to get their attention, God still talks to them. He still affirms his love for them.*

GRACE, NOT KARMA

Say: *Nothing could be further from how God views things than this notion of a bank account of a person's deeds. What have we seen so far in the study of Ezekiel about what God is most interested in?* God is interested in the state of your heart today.

• Reread verses 21-24 to your students. Ask: *What do these verses tell us about God's view of the "bank account"?*
• *What if you're rebelling against God right now? Will it count in your favor that your parents had you baptized as a baby? Or that you used to go to church all the time as a kid and have a reward somewhere in your mom's basement for all the Bible verses you memorized? What about if you're* not *rebelling right now?*
• Explain: *But the reverse is true, too: If you've never done anything for God and messed up in every way imaginable before you turned to him, he will erase all of that*

[16] Block, *The Book of Ezekiel: Chapters 1-24*, 585.

past and give newness of life so you can start over. The point is, God wants a relationship with you, and he cares about the ongoing relationship and the state of your heart.

YOU SHOULD BE DEAD

Conclude: *According to this chapter, the soul who sins dies. By that measurement, we all deserve to be dead. Does that change how we think about what God "should" be doing? Or at least, what he "could" be doing?*

In all fairness, none of us deserves a relationship with God, a second chance, the right to be happy, to live a good life—anything. Fair would be getting what we deserved, which would be eternal death and separation from God. So is God not fair?

Explain: *Somehow the penalty for sin had to be paid, or else God wouldn't be just. So what does he do? Instead of making us pay it, he pays it for us and then offers us the gift of new life in him—for all eternity. So the next time we're tempted to say that life's not fair…go ahead and say it! But be very, very thankful that it's not. Fair would leave none of us here.*

So what should God be doing? I don't know, but I know I can trust him, and while I'll never completely understand him, the fact that God's already given us so much that we don't deserve makes me confident of his goodness. That—and the fact that God continues to pursue us even when we're running from him because he's trying to offer us the gift of a relationship with him and new life—blows my mind. The God who created the universe and all we know is personally chasing us because he's passionately in love with us. Wow!

CLOSING

Pass out the journaling exercise, **The Hound of Heaven**. The late-19th-century poem, "The Hound of Heaven," expresses beautifully the poet's experience of trying to run away from God and how this "tremendous Lover" (line 32) wouldn't give up on him but continued to pursue him and tell him of his unfailing love (lines 50-79). This poem would make an excellent reflection for your students during the journaling time. (You can print a version of the poem via various Internet sites; there's an abridged version courtesy of www2.bc.edu/~anderso/sr/ft.html that I found helpful.)

JOURNALING: THE HOUND OF HEAVEN

Think of an incident in which God didn't do what you expected him to do. Write a note or a symbol here that represents that event to you.

Do you think you form or have formed views of God based on whether or not he did what you expected him to do? Why or why not?

What do you think about views of God, based on this session?

Have any of the views related been close to views you've held? Which ones and why?

Write to God and tell him what you're thinking right now…

CONTRACTS, COVENANTS, AND CHOCOLATE CHIP COOKIES

SESSION 8: EZEKIEL 20:1-29, 44; ROMANS 3:26

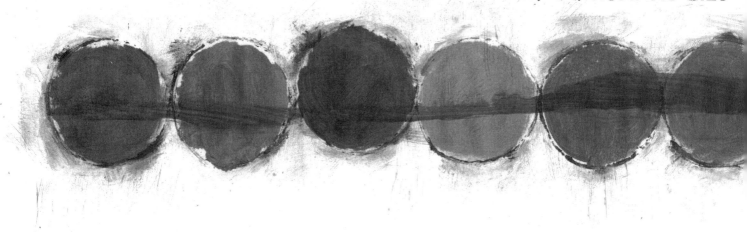

OVERVIEW

We've all broken promises to God and sinned against him. There's nothing we can do to rescue ourselves, so we must return to our God, whose heart we have broken, and ask for his mercy and grace. It's hard for us to do because of our pride, but in reality, this is exactly what God longs for us to do. This session will explain to your students the nature of a broken covenant and give them an opportunity to renew their own covenants with God. The idea is to have them understand the serious nature of making a promise to God, and then allow space for them to experience the joy of making things right with God.

SET UP

ILLUSTRATION

• "Cookies" baked with only half the ingredients

ACTIVITY

• Three decks of playing cards (remove the king of hearts from each deck and shuffle the three decks together.)

COMMUNION

• Pens and pieces of paper

• A communion table, preferably with candles, set up in the front of the room[17]

• A cross placed in the front of the room, if possible

• A trash can or some kind of bin or container into which the students can throw paper before they reach the communion table (Having the table up front the entire time provides a sacred atmosphere for this serious topic.)

SONGS

• "The Heart of Worship," Matt Redman (*The Heart of Worship*, 1999)

• "Here Is Our King," David Crowder Band (*A Collision*, 2005)

• "Blessed Be Your Name," Matt Redman (*Blessed Be Your Name, The Songs of Matt Redman, Vol. 1*, 2005)

SECTION 1: BACKGROUND FOR LEADERS

EZEKIEL 20: FOR THE SAKE OF MY NAME

Here in Ezekiel 20, we find a broken covenant.

A covenant contains six main parts, according to the traditions of Ezekiel's day and even before that. As we look at them, what God had done, and what the people had done, imagine what this chapter would say if God had addressed it to you instead of to the nation of Israel. You see, God is arraigning them here. *Arraign* is a legal term that means to bring a case against someone. Where verse 4 reads *judge*, the word could also be read as *arraign*. God is acting as both prosecutor and judge in this chapter, in effect saying, "Here's what Israel has done wrong—here's where she has broken the covenant." And he's also saying, "Here's what she deserves, and here's how I'm going to treat her."

[17] Aven, *Nelson's Annual Sourcebook for Youth Ministers*, 248-53.

THE PRINCIPAL PARTS OF A COVENANT ARE:

1. **The preamble**: Ezekiel 20:3. Who are the people involved? In this case, it's God; so who is God? He's the Sovereign LORD. *Sovereign* means supreme: "superlative in strength or efficacy."[18] That means God's in charge; the most powerful; the most effective in whatever he does. And this all-powerful being, the same one Ezekiel saw coming in glory in the first session of this book, says in verse 5, "I am the LORD *your* God." He has chosen to be identified first with Israel, and now with us, his church. He is *our* God. The creator of this world is *our* God.

2. **A history of the relationship**: Ezekiel 20:4-7. Where have they been? God brought the Israelites out of Egypt. This was a major deal. He not only delivered them—set them free—but showed anyone, any nation, watching who God is as well. How has God delivered you and set you free? Who's watching you and getting a picture of who God is because of what he's done in your life?

3. **A declaration about the future relationship of the partners**: Ezekiel 20:8-22. This is where the covenant partners' ideal future is supposed to be. Although this chapter isn't a covenant, it follows the covenant form and shows how Israel has broken the covenant. This section goes back and forth between what God said he would do, what the Israelites did, and what God should do in response.

Here we find three repetitions: (1) In verses 8 and 9, after the LORD told the Israelites to leave behind the idols of Egypt, (2) in verses 13 and 14, after the LORD had told Israel in the desert to keep the Sabbath as a sign between himself and them so they would know "I the LORD made them holy," and (3) the second generation of people in the desert rebelled, worshiped idols, and didn't keep God's laws or his Sabbath as a sign between them (verses 21-22). Because the covenant had been broken, God says what he should do in the future as a result, but doesn't because of his name's sake.

Why is it so important to God to act according to his name's sake? It says in verse 9 that God revealed himself to Israel in the sight of the nations around Israel, and thus did not want his name "profaned" by those people. If God wiped out the nation of Israel in the sight of the other nations after rescuing her, the other nations wouldn't have ever respected or potentially worshiped God. Therefore God acted for his own witness to the other nations; God acted in line with his character and for the sake of his reputation. God's actions on behalf of Israel were very public, and everyone around her knew Israel was in a covenant with this God.

4. **Details of the new relationship**: Ezekiel 20:21-29. It's different here again because the people aren't keeping the covenant. They're going against everything the LORD had told them to do. What exactly was God so upset about? Here we read their offenses: Worshiping idols and not keeping the Sabbath. What's with the first one? Israel was cheating on God by worshiping idols. He was supposed to be her first love. This covenant language used throughout the Bible is very much akin to a marriage covenant. Israel had done the equivalent of a bride marrying a husband, and then running off and sleeping around. It was bad, and it was serious. God was brokenhearted and angry, just as a husband who discovered his wife had been cheating on him would be brokenhearted and angry.

The other main issue God has with Israel is that she "desecrated his Sabbaths." *Desecrate* means to "violate the sacredness of." This is a really strong word. God had

---

[18] *Webster's II New Riverside University Dictionary*, 1112.

given them a sacred gift. What was the Sabbath after all? A day of rest. So what's the big deal? They were violating a day of rest. Seems as though there are worse sins. But this day was supposed to be a symbol that the LORD had made them holy (verse 12). By not doing any work on that day, they were acknowledging that God was their provider and their holiness. Do we take enough time in our lives to acknowledge God as our provider, or are we constantly running from one thing to the next, doing it all on our own? Are we frantic in our pace because there's simply one more thing that absolutely has to be done?

5. **Calling on the gods worshiped by both parties**: In this case, the one and only God is one of the parties, and he brings up his name throughout this chapter, especially in verses 9, 14, 22, and 44.

6. **A pronouncement of curse and blessing**: Three times it says Israel rebelled against God (verses 8, 13, and 21); three times God says he should pour out his wrath (i.e., the curse, verses 8, 13, and 21); and four times God says he will deal with them for his name's sake (verses 9, 14, 22, and 44).

SECTION 2: MAKING IT LIVE FOR YOUR STUDENTS

INTRODUCTION: HOW DO YOU FIX A BROKEN PROMISE?

ILLUSTRATION: NEW YEAR'S DAY AND THE CLEAN SLATE

- *Think back to last New Year's Day.*
- *Do you like New Year's Day? Why or why not?*
- *What kind of resolutions did you make?*
- *How long did the resolutions last?*

Explain: *Lots of people love New Year's Day. I like it, too, but it's not nearly as big a deal to me as it is to some. I was thinking about why that might be. You see, New Year's is the time when people feel like they can start over. It's a clean slate. If you think hard enough, maybe it even seems like all your mistakes are behind you—part of the old year, not the new, and you'll never make those mistakes again. Never. After all, it's a new year. The parallel to salvation is clear here. When people accept Jesus, all things become new, right? Or do they?*

- *Without naming names, has someone ever broken a promise to you? How did that feel?*

- *Have you ever made a promise to God you didn't keep?* Don't ask for explicit answers or examples.

- *I'd guess that just about every one of you has probably prayed when you're stuck in a jam, "Lord, if you'll just get me out of this, I'll…" Fill in the blank. We've all done it.*

DIGGING IN: WHAT DID YOU SIGN UP FOR WHEN YOU BECAME A CHRISTIAN?

• *Who here has installed something on a computer before?*

• *When you install a new program, what sort of options are you given?* When you install a new program, you're often presented with options regarding how much you want to install—the basic version, the help files, the advanced-user items, and so forth. That way, the program doesn't take up as much space on your hard drive; you get to choose how much space it occupies.

• Explain: *A lot of times when people accept Jesus, they want to install him into their lives with a menu full of options. They want to choose how much space he takes up in their hearts. They want the eternal-life component, the get-me-out-of-trouble-when-I-pray component—you know, the "help file" that instantly responds when we click on the "Help, Lord!" icon. They want the comfort, joy, and peace parts, but a lot of people aren't really sure how much of the holy lifestyle, the unconditional-surrender-to-God's-will part they want. Oh sure, some of it's there, but how much? God has revealed himself to any who will look and in doing so has offered the possibility of a special relationship with him for any who will accept it.*

• *What did you sign up for when you became a Christian?* This is more of a rhetorical question, so just pause after you ask this and then go on to the next concept.

The Israelites liked this idea of a partial installation. They liked the idea of God's protection, God's guidance, provided of course that he guided them out of trouble and not into anything scary. You see, they wanted a partial covenant. They didn't want all of the space in their lives taken up with God.

What exactly is a covenant? What is this term? It's not something we hear all that often these days. We often hear the word contract, but a covenant and a contract aren't the same thing.

CHOCOLATE CHIP COOKIES

Bring in "cookies" that are made from half of the ingredients. Get a cookie recipe and take out some of the essential ingredients such as the baking soda, the chocolate chips, and so forth. Mix them up as you would cookies; then instead of trying to drop them on a cookie sheet, put the mixture in a glass baking pan and bake until it looks solid. Then cut it up like "bars." Pass them around and have the students try them.

• Explain: *A contract is like this: Let's say I want to bake chocolate chip cookies. I go to my cabinet and discover I have exactly half of the ingredients. I have flour, but no sugar, and so forth. So, I go to my neighbor's house and tell her my dilemma. Well, it just so happens that she wants to make chocolate chip cookies, too, but she only has half the ingredients—and as a matter of fact, the half I'm missing. So, we enter into a contract that states we will bake chocolate chip cookies together and evenly split the batch of cookies. Now, if one of us fails to show up with our ingredients, then there can be no cookies. That's a contract.*

• But God makes covenants with his people. Back to our cookie analogy: God decides to bake cookies, so he goes and gets all the ingredients, mixes up the cookie dough, bakes the cookies, and then says, "Here, to be a part of this covenant, you have to eat this cookie." Pretty cool—God does it all. But we have to accept the covenant on God's terms. That means we have to eat the whole cookie. We can't just pick out the chocolate chips of grace, forgiveness, and happiness; we also need to swallow the holiness parts, the surrender parts, and the living-in-God's-will parts. How did the incomplete chocolate-chip cookies taste to you? Not very good. See? Chocolate chip cookies taste best when they're eaten whole. So does God's covenant. It works best in your life when you install the whole package.

Briefly explain how Ezekiel 20 represents a covenant turned on its head. How much of the Background for Leaders section you wish to include depends on the age of your kids, as well as their spiritual maturity to some extent.

Say: *Sometimes, we think we can be good enough for God, but only God can renew a covenant we have broken. Here is an activity that helps illustrate the futility of trying to fix the broken promises on our own.*

ONE HUNDRED AND FIFTEEN PICKUP

You'll need three decks of cards. Remove the king of hearts from each deck.

• Shuffle the three decks together.

• Pick three teams and three team captains.

• Divide the cards among the teams.

• Tell the students that in order to make a complete deck of cards, they need to trade with the other teams to get the cards they need. Give the team captains two minutes to divide the teams into seekers (who go trade the cards) and organizers (who put them together and give the seekers the extra cards).

• Have the students organize the cards into suits in hopes of seeing if the decks are complete. The idea is that they have to work with the other teams in order to get the cards they need. Once they figure out which cards are extras, they'll trade those with the other teams.

• Two points are made here: (1) The process of putting the cards together is like a contract. Everyone has to fulfill his or her parts or the project is impossible. (2) The decks are incomplete without the king of hearts—God. Human contracts and attempts will always be empty without God, and to have God, we have to meet him on his terms—not ours.

Read Ezekiel 20:44. Here's a suggested summary: *God will deal with Israel, who had broken her promises to him, for his name's sake, not because of anything Israel could do to "make it up" to him. We've all broken promises to God. We've all broken his heart. And there's nothing we can do to make it up to him—we have to go back to God and allow him to fix what was broken. Our part is simply going back to God. It can be pretty scary going to someone you've wronged to ask for forgiveness, especially when it's the living God. But you have to go to God, knowing you've broken his heart, and ask him to forgive you. But this is what God is longing for you to do.*

CLOSING

Have your worship team play something meditative like "The Heart of Worship" by Matt Redman (*The Heart of Worship*, 1999) or simply play the song on a stereo. Pass out the journaling exercise, **Broken Promises**, as well as sheets of blank paper and pens. Ask your students to set aside the journaling sheet; then invite them to spread out and write down the promises they've made to God and broken—things they haven't dealt with before God. Turn the lights down to offer some privacy (but leave them high enough to write) and leave time for them to meet God, at least five minutes for junior highers and 10 for high schoolers. Make it clear that no one will read what they write down—this is between them and God. You might suggest that they use personal abbreviations, or even just think of incidents and use the paper as a symbol of those times.

Leave the lights down, but walk back up front. Tell them the story doesn't end here. Read them the following conclusion adapted from the Background for Leaders pages, but put it into your own words.

Only God can renew the covenant broken by human disobedience. Why did God think it was so important to do things the way he said they should be done? The answer to that question is in Ezekiel 20:11: "The man who obeys [God's laws] will live by them." God's commandments are the way to life. This is the blessing made possible by the covenant. However, we have broken the covenant and can't get back to God. Even as Christians, we can't "make up" for our sin. What happens next?

God sums up the covenant in Ezekiel 36:28 when he promises: "You will be my people, and I will be your God." Exodus 6:7 says this: "I will take you as my own people, and I will be your God. Then you will know that I am the Lord *your God, who brought you out from under the yoke of the Egyptians." To us, the words of the covenant may sound more like Romans 3:26: "He did it [died on the cross] to demonstrate his justice at the present time, so as to be just and the one who justifies those who have faith in Jesus." We find this same idea in Ezekiel. Jesus died for us, not because we've somehow earned it or deserved it, but because he is just. Some penalty had to be paid for sin. God acted in line with his character by dying for our sins, just as God was in line with his character in Ezekiel when he acted for the sake of his name and honor. Because of God's great love for his people, God also chose not to wipe out all of humankind for what they had done, but rather to offer them a way out of the penalty of sin.*

The Sovereign Lord, *Creator of all, the King of Kings, was broken for you. When you asked Jesus into your heart, you accepted his covenant. The question that now lies before you is, "How much of that covenant are you keeping?" Are there idols in your life—things you put in front of or even in place of God? Are you allowing yourself to feel good about your Christian life because of the good things you've done, rather than knowing that holiness is from God alone?*

What will you do with this broken King? What is the call of the broken King on your life? Jesus will forever bear the marks on his body of the covenant he kept; will you forever bear the mark of the covenant in your life? What difference does being in covenant with the living God make in your life? What difference does it make to call yourself a Christian?

CLOSING: COMMUNION

Prepare your students for communion by telling them communion is all about new promises and new covenants.
• Read 1 Corinthians 11:23-26.
• If you have real bread (or matzo wafers), break it while you read the passage; it will help flesh out the concepts for your students.
• Then have them come up a few at a time, throw away their list of broken promises in a bin up by the communion table, and get the bread and wine/grape juice.
• Explain: *Today is your "New Year's," and you can start over with a clean slate.*
• Inviting any non-Christians in the group to accept Jesus would be appropriate here.

Encourage your students to write in their journals, using the handout as a guide after they've taken communion.

Then when they're done, end with a song of celebration, such as "Blessed Be Your Name" by Matt Redman (*Blessed Be Your Name, The Songs of Matt Redman, Vol. 1,* 2005) or "Here Is Our King" by David Crowder Band (*A Collision,* 2005; you can get these songs from iTunes for $0.99 each).

JOURNALING: BROKEN PROMISES

Did tonight's meeting do anything for you? Explain.

What does it mean for you to know that Jesus has made a way for you to have a relationship with him, and regardless of how many times you've walked away, you can walk back tonight?

Tell God about the state of your heart right now and what you're thinking…

WHEN GOD COMES LOOKING FOR YOU
SESSION 9: EZEKIEL 34:11-16; 36:22-28; PSALM 139

OVERVIEW

Previous chapters have covered the idea that God goes with his people and takes great pains to get them to return to him. Ezekiel 34 uses the imagery of a shepherd looking for his sheep. God continually closes the distance between us and him; however, it's still up to us to respond to God. But, if you were planning on running from God, he's really good at keeping track of you regardless of where you go (Psalm 139). He will continually call to you; what will be your response?

SET UP

MUSIC VIDEO OR SONG

• "Meant to Live," Switchfoot (*The Beautiful Letdown*, 2003)

SONG:

• "The Way I Was Made," Chris Tomlin (*Arriving*, 2004)

MOVIE:

The Chronicles of Narnia: The Lion, the Witch and the Wardrobe

SECTION 1: BACKGROUND FOR LEADERS

CONTEXT OF EZEKIEL 34:11-16; 36:22-28 IN THE WHOLE OF THE BOOK

Since session 8, which covered Ezekiel 20, we have now jumped to chapter 34. What happens between these two chapters is a further and extremely graphic description of Israel and Judah's sins and adultery (see chapters 22-23), more sign acts about the fall of Jerusalem (see chapter 24), and then a series of oracles against other nations that have persecuted Israel (see chapters 25-32). The oracles against the other nations list their offenses against Israel and detail their judgment. These are important pieces of the book, especially in terms of historical significance and understanding a complete picture of what was going on in the time this was written in terms of the major players. However, I've omitted them in this study because we're covering Ezekiel in 12 sessions, so we must find a theme to pull out. In light of the fact that we've thoroughly examined God's judgment on those who rebel against him and what that means for our lives, getting into each of these oracles would be somewhat redundant. Therefore, what follows from here on out is a theme of redemption and restoration—prophecies of the new life God wants to bring to all of us if we'll choose it (for more on this idea, see the Nations Versus Individuals section).

CONTEXT IN THE TIMELINE

In Ezekiel 33:21, we're given a date: the fifth day of the 10th month in the 12th year of the exile. This date would be January 8, 585 BC.[19] At this point in Ezekiel, it's seven and a half years from the beginning of the book and a little less than five months after the temple was burned in Jerusalem in August of 586 BC (2 Kings 25:8). These dates are fairly accurate within a year or so. The most often quoted possible date for the fall of Jerusalem is either in 587 or 586 BC. Based on the first two dates, the fall of Jerusalem would have occurred in July of 586 BC. So, give or take a year, this gives us an idea of the book's chronology. After Ezekiel hears about the fall of Jerusalem on that day in January of 585 BC, the emphasis of his prophecies turns toward the restoration of Israel. First God will look for her in order to heal her and bring her back, and that's where we'll pick up the story as it applies to our lives.

[19] See note on Ezekiel 33:21 in the NIV Study Bible.

HEALING THE WOUNDS

God is promising to gather the people and pasture them back in their own land, removing any obstacles to their security. God himself will tend this flock, binding up the wounds of the injured and strengthening the weak. God promises to protect them from bullies in the flock who have made themselves sleek and strong at the expense of the weak (34:16). These strong sheep have ruined the pasture and muddied the waters (verse 18) after they've eaten and drunk their fill so that no one else can take advantage of the pasture. And God will judge the strong sheep for butting the weak sheep away. This is part of ensuring his flock's security (verse 22), making sure they could sleep in peace (verse 25), and ensuring they would have all the food they needed (verse 27). God is also going to restore the covenant of peace (verse 25) so that "they will live in safety, and no one will make them afraid" (verse 28). The result of all of this is that Israel will know "that I, the LORD their God, am with them and that they, the house of Israel, are my people, declares the Sovereign LORD. You my sheep, the sheep of my pasture, are people, and I am your God, declares the Sovereign LORD" (verses 30-31).

WHY DO WE RUN FROM GOD WHEN HE HAS A PLAN TO RESTORE US?

Where in our lives are we wounded by our past? Where have we lost our strength? Is it hard to sleep in peace because of the consequences of our actions? Are we not exactly provided for because of where we've gotten ourselves? There is good news. We have a shepherd, and he is pursuing us. And even if we believe we can get away from God, we can't. Psalm 139 provides a wonderful picture of God searching and knowing us (verse 1). God is intimately acquainted with everything we do (verses 2-4) and has hemmed us in behind and before (verse 5). The psalmist is staggered by this knowledge, as well as the realization that there is nowhere to go to flee from God's presence. There is no place high enough, deep enough, far enough, or dark enough to hide us from the living God who will never stop his pursuit of us (verses 7-12).

After all, God created us, knitting us together with his own hands (verses 13 and 15) and making us in his image, and he has a plan for us that was written before we were even born (verse 16). And the offer God extends to us is an offer to make us clean and to give us a new heart and a new spirit (Ezekiel 36:25-26). Here in the second passage we're looking at today, God is promising to make us clean and new regardless of what we've done.

NATIONS VERSUS INDIVIDUALS

It's important to realize that although we're applying Ezekiel's words from God to individual people, this book has a historical context and is directed at a nation. As we've seen in Ezekiel 7, there is interplay between what God is saying about the nation and what God is saying about the individual. Ezekiel 34:11-31 is about the fact that God is going to bring Israel back. This restoration is not contingent upon human response. There is no call to repentance here. But how can God restore Israel without repentance? Here God is acting for the sake of his name among the nations so they'll see that he is holy, that he is God. Walter Brueggemann points out that by acting for the sake of his name, God roots the new beginning in himself rather than in the actions of the nation of Israel. "Now the possibility of land is exclusively Yahweh's initiative."[20]

You might say God has a grand scheme for the restoration of the world, just as he had a grand scheme for the restoration of Israel. Now whether you and I as individuals opt into this grand scheme, in which his kingdom purposes come to fruition, is entirely up to us. Keeping these distinctions between what God is doing on a large scale and what God is doing on an individual scale is vital, or else it ends up looking like God's actions are deterministic on the individual level and thus remove the element of choice.

SECTION 2: MAKING IT LIVE FOR YOUR STUDENTS

INTRODUCTION: RUNNING FROM WHAT'S GOOD FOR YOU

Ask your students: *Remember when you were a little kid and you didn't want to take your medicine or your vitamins? Or you didn't want to go down for a nap when your parents said it was time? Or you wished you could just eat candy, cookies, and dessert and not any "good" food? How often did we fight our parents over stuff they were trying to do for our own good? How about when we scraped a knee or an elbow and they whipped out the dreaded hydrogen peroxide, and we yelled that they were hurting us? Which, of course, they were—hydrogen peroxide stings like no other. But if they didn't clean it, then what would have happened? Now that we're older, we can see they were only doing it to help us. But it sure might not have seemed like it at the time…*

This sort of thing is what God was dealing with when he was restoring the nation of Israel. They were running from him still, and he was pursuing them. Why? Because he wanted to bind up their wounds, heal them, and bring them back to their homeland.

DIGGING IN: LOOKING FOR STRAYS

Read Ezekiel 34:11-16 with your students. Select several volunteers to each read a verse or two.

• *What are some words you hear repeated in this passage?* Students should pull out the shepherd concept.

20 Brueggemann. *The Land*, 132.

• *Who is the shepherd?* This passage (Ezekiel 34:11-16) depicts God as the shepherd looking for his sheep.

• Explain: *This passage takes place after the fall of Jerusalem.*

• Summarize: *Israel had suffered a "day of clouds and darkness" (verse 12) when Jerusalem fell, and she was ultimately scattered even more than had already taken place in the exile. I think many of us can relate to having a day or days of clouds and darkness—you know, those days or time periods when nothing seems to go right? You see, Jerusalem was a symbol of hope for the exiles. As long as Jerusalem stood, there was a place to call home.*

• *Can you imagine what it must have been like to know that your home had fallen? Picture yourself in a foreign country, and you get the news that your home has been destroyed. How would you feel?* Pick up on words from your students that lead to feeling hopeless, discouraged, sad…any of those negative "down" emotions.

• *When the city fell, those hopes were shattered. This happens to us, too, when we discover that in the middle of all the other things going on in the mess that is often our lives, it seems as though there's no going back, and there's no going home. Perhaps home has been shattered due to any multitude of reasons that may or may not be part of what we've done to mess up our own lives. But regardless, home is gone, and with it goes the hope of ever feeling like there's a place to belong again. Or does it?*

• Ask: *Who do you think the sheep in this passage represent?* The people of Israel have been scattered all over, to multiple countries, and are anywhere but where God wants them to be, so he goes looking for them to bring them back.

• *Imagine you are scattered far away from your home and there's no way you can get home by yourself. How would it feel to hear God say: "I myself will search for my sheep" (verse 11)?*

• *What condition were some of the sheep in (verse 16)?* Weak, sick, injured, and some of them had strayed.

• *Since these sheep represent the people of Israel, how do you think these sheep/people were injured, sick, weak, and scattered all over the place?* They had walked out of God's covenant and care of them and thus opened themselves up to all sorts of pain and injury.

• *Is the sheep's location important in order for God to bring them back?* No, God can find them (and can find you) wherever they are.

• *Does the condition of the sheep make a difference as to whether God finds them? Why?* No, the condition doesn't matter because God can restore us, heal us, and bring us into the life we were meant to live.

Say: *See, just as we discussed in session 7, God would be the sanctuary to the exiles in the foreign land (11:16). God himself is home for them* and *for us, regardless of the physical place we're in. What's more, in this promise of restoration, we discover that God can bring us home, restore what's been lost, and breathe new life into us.*

MOVIE CLIP (OR BOOK EXCERPT): *THE CHRONICLES OF NARNIA - THE LION, THE WITCH AND THE WARDROBE—GOD'S LOVE IN ACTION*

Play clip 1. START [00:29:42] STOP [00:34:07]

• Ask: *In* The Lion, the Witch and the Wardrobe, *why does Edmond want the Turkish delight so badly? What is he willing to do to get it?* The witch feeds him enchanted Turkish delight, and all he can think of is how he wants more and more of it, to the point where he's willing to betray his brother and sisters to get more.

• *What does the witch promise Edmund?* She promises she will adopt him and make him the prince so he will be king one day.

• *Is there a catch to what the witch promises Edmund?* He has to bring his sisters and brother to her.

Play clip 2. START [01:31:46] STOP [01:33:33] (Chapter 16: The witch comes to Aslan's camp to bargain for Edmund's life.)

• *Why did the witch believe she had the right to march into Aslan's camp and demand Edmund's life?*

Play clip 3. START [01:53:15] STOP [01:54:33] (Aslan's resurrection and explanation of the deeper magic)

• *Someone summarize what happened right before this scene in the movie.* Get your students to explain that Aslan lays down his life in Edmund's place.

• *Does this scenario sound familiar? Where else do we see something like this happen?* Make sure they draw the parallels back to what Jesus did for us.

• Ask: *What did Aslan owe Edmund?* Nothing.

• *What kind of relationship did Aslan and Edmund have before this?* Up until he was rescued from the witch, Edmund had never even met Aslan. *This is a great illustration of God's plan being in effect before we even know that it is. Aslan is willing to give up his life to save that of a boy who hardly knows him and who doesn't know what it will cost Aslan. Jesus gave up his life for us long before we were even born.*

• *What did he owe us?* Nothing.

• *And he still owes us nothing. Jesus offered himself because it's his nature to offer himself. The question then is, what are we going to do with his offer?*

See, once we understand God is at work in our world and is bringing about his purposes in our world, even when we don't understand him, we have a choice to make: Are we going to opt into his plan?

God's overall purposes for the world in all of time will be completed. He's God and has the power to bring that about. The question is whether or not you'll be included in God's plan—and that decision is entirely up to you.

Now, does God have a place for you? Have a student read Psalm 139:16 in the NLT (mark this passage in a Bible before the meeting so you can just pass the volunteer a marked Bible).

• *What is the significance of the statement, "Every day of my life was recorded in your book"?* God's plan is there for every day of your life.

• *How detailed is God's plan according to this verse?* Every minute is covered.

OPTING INTO GOD'S GRAND SCHEME

Tell your students the following story. If you need to read it out loud, that's fine; just make sure they know that the "I" isn't you.

Once when I was about 17, I was on a family trip in England. We visited this wonderful old castle that had a maze made out of bushes. And yes, it looked a lot like the one in Harry Potter and the Goblet of Fire, *if you've seen that movie. Thankfully, the walls in this one didn't move on us, but that didn't make life much easier on us. See, the bushes were a good 10 feet tall and had been very well maintained, so any holes were hardly big enough to do us any good. We were very lost within about five minutes, and we kept ending up back in the front left corner somehow, even though we'd tried everything from leaving broken twigs in the paths we'd gone down to memorizing how many turns we'd taken where.*

Now the objective in the maze was to get to the center, which was a small hill, and you could see it from certain parts of the maze, but even that wasn't helping us get any closer to it. Finally, after wandering around for quite a while, we discovered we were one bush's width away from the entrance where we'd started. Now that wouldn't have done us any good because there was no getting through these bushes to get out, but the old gardener happened to be standing there trimming some of the bushes. So we humbly asked him if he could give us some pointers. He told us to walk to the end of the row, take a left, and then an immediate right, and then keep heading left or something like that, so we did. Within about five minutes, we'd reached the center of the maze. We climbed to the top feeling rather triumphant and looked down at all the poor people still stuck in the maze.

A guy was standing on top, who had gotten up a little before we had, and he spotted his friends in the maze. He yelled and got their attention and then starting telling them which way to go and what turns to make, because he could see which path would lead them to the middle. He talked them through it, and then we all climbed down into a tunnel in the hill and went out to the free air.

Now for both us and the other guy's friends who were lost in the maze, it made a lot of sense to listen to people who knew what they were talking about. See, both the gardener and the guy at the top had been through the maze. In the gardener's case, he probably knew it backward and forward because he worked there every day. For the guy who had made it to the top, even though he didn't know it as well as the gardener, he could see the path where the people were walking.

• *What do you think would have happened if the people in the story didn't listen to the gardener?*

• *Why did it make sense to follow the gardener's directions or listen to the dude on the top?* Because they had been there and knew the path.

• *What similarities can we draw from this story about the maze to our lives?* Life can be confusing, and we don't know where we should go next. It helps to have someone who's walked the path before to tell us where to go next.

• *So, in our lives, who is the gardener or the dude on top giving directions?*

• *This passage we've just studied gives us a great picture of God's love for us.*

• *Given that God loves us, what do you think is God's motivation for having a step-by-step plan to follow?* He wants what is best for us.

Have a student read Ezekiel 36:33-36.

• *What are the promises in this passage?*

• *Remember, Jerusalem had fallen, and the people would have felt hopeless with no home to return to. What do you think would be the most exciting thing for them to hear?* That their homes would be rebuilt, which is what God promises in this passage.

In closing, say: *So here we have it. Understanding that God is on a mission to restore is a message that should bring huge doses of hope into whatever situation we find ourselves in. Whether or not it will provide hope depends on us. God will continue to pursue us no matter where we go because he loves us that much. The question is, will we opt into his plan?*

CLOSING

Pass out the journaling exercise, **We Were Meant to Live for So Much More**. Encourage your students to write to God about where they are and what they think about opting into his scheme and giving him their lives. Play "Meant to Live" by Switchfoot (*Beautiful Letdown*, 2003) while the students journal. If you have PowerPoint capability, create a presentation with the lyrics and perhaps some nature photos. (If you don't have photos for worship presentations, check out www.sxc.hu, which is a free stock-photography site where you can download all sorts of creative photos. Some of them require permission from the artist, but most of them don't. Check restrictions at the bottom of the photo.) Having the PowerPoint (or MediaShout) images playing along with the song creates an atmosphere to "surround" the students with the lyrics in a sense. Or you could play the music video of "Meant to Live."

For a closing song, singing "The Way I Was Made" by Chris Tomlin (*Arriving*, 2004) would be appropriate. (You can get these songs or the video from iTunes for $0.99/song or $1.99/video.)

JOURNALING: WE WERE MEANT TO LIVE FOR SO MUCH MORE

We as humans were meant to live in relationship with God. That is how we are the most satisfied. But somehow, we've forgotten that, and, in fact, we often run from what he's doing because we're afraid it will hurt us.

Can you think of a time in your life when something you were sure was going to be a bad thing turned out to be something good—and then you realized God was working for your good in it? Write a note to yourself so you'll remember when that was.

What does it mean for you to turn your life over to God? Is that a step you're ready to take? Why or why not?

What do you suppose opting into God's plan looks like for you? Talk to God about what you think this means and write out what you're praying…

CAN MY DEAD LIFE LIVE AGAIN?
SESSION 10: EZEKIEL 37:1-14; PSALM 139:13-16

OVERVIEW

So what happens when you run from God and everything gets so messed up that you can't see how anything good could possibly come from your life ever again? Just as God brings an army of dry bones to life in Ezekiel 37, he can resurrect and reconstruct the pieces of your life. After all, he created you and had a plan for your life before you were even born (Psalm 139:13-16).

SET UP

GAME (MAKE SURE YOU READ THE GAME INSTRUCTIONS BEFORE GETTING SUPPLIES)

• A package of disposable plastic bathroom cups

• Compressed towels (one capsule per 10 students)

• Baking pans (one per 10 students)

• Buckets or bowls (one per 10 students)

- Chairs (two per 10 students)
- Masking tape

MUSIC VIDEO

- "The Scientist," Coldplay (*A Rush of Blood to the Head*, 2002)

SONG

- "There Is a Redeemer," Keith Green (*Songs for the Shepherd*, 1986)

SECTION 1: BACKGROUND FOR LEADERS

WHEN THINGS ARE DEAD

We've spent all this time looking at the exile and God's attempts to get the people's attention and bring them back to their land. I still am struck by the fact that I can even say "God's attempts." This is the all-powerful Creator who spoke the world into existence, and the one and only instance when we could say he "attempts" to do something, rather than just speaking it into existence, is when it comes to winning our hearts. That's how powerful God's commitment to relationships is. And God goes through the trouble of going into exile with his people because exile was both a result of the Israelites' sin and an attempt to produce certain results. See, exile is not death. You can't come back from the dead, but you can come back from exile, even though at this point in the book of Ezekiel, his audience probably felt like there was no going back.

Jerusalem had fallen. It was over. Hope was gone—end of story, finished. The people were saying, "Our bones are dried up and our hope is gone; we are cut off" (Ezekiel 37:11). But it isn't over for God. You see, "Things that seem hopelessly lost, closed, and dead are the very region of God's new action. The reversal of destiny is not some clever trick of human ingenuity, but it is the action of God himself when all human ingenuity has failed. Nor is the reversal of destiny some psychological or spiritual change, but it is the radical transformation of a historical, political situation."[21] Know this: Our God is into reversal of destiny. Even when it looks like things are hopeless, dead, and finished, the story doesn't end there.

WHERE LIFE COMES FROM

In Ezekiel's prophecy, we see a two-step resuscitation: Block suggests that the force of these two steps is in the fact that (1) the pause emphasizes the fact that these

[21] Brueggemann, *The Land*, 126.
[22] Block, *The Book of Ezekiel: Chapters 25-48*, 379.

bones live only because the LORD has infused them with life, and (2) it recalls the creation narrative in Genesis 2:7, when God makes Adam from the clay, but he doesn't live until God breathes into him.[22]

So what do these two steps mean for us? Earlier in the chapter, we see that our resuscitation comes from throwing ourselves on God's mercy and recognizing that only he can bring back that which is lost and dead. Here we see God is also the source of all life (Ecclesiastes 12:7), and we only live because he breathes his breath of life into us.[23]

Walking away from the source of life leads to death, as Israel has now experienced in both the exile and the fall of Jerusalem. She just didn't realize why walking away from God leads to death, but if you think about it, it's quite clear. If we walk away from God—our source of life—we'll die just as surely as the person dependent on dragging his oxygen tank around will die if he removes his nosepiece and walks away from his tank. Who would do that? It's stupid, right? But then again, so is walking away from God. We can't live without him. After all, God created our inmost being and knit us together in our mothers' wombs (Psalm 139:13), and God knows every intricate detail of us intimately. He has a plan for us, if only we'll simply say, "You alone know how to help me," thus throwing ourselves at his feet and into his hands so God can work with us.

SECTION 2: MAKING IT LIVE FOR YOUR STUDENTS

GAME: CAN THE DEAD TOWEL LIVE?

NOTE: Test one of the compressed-towel capsules to see how fast it responds and how much water it uses. If it's going too fast or too slow with repeated doses from the bathroom cups, adjust your container size to either larger cups or something smaller, on down to an eyedropper.

Before the meeting:

• Clear out part of your youth room so you have 20 to 30 feet for students to run back and forth.

• Create a line on your floor with masking tape, leaving room for lines of 10 students behind it (see diagram).

• Set up two chairs for every 10 students, one on one side of the room, and one on the opposite side (see diagram).

• Fill up the bowls with water and place them on the chairs nearest to the lines of students.

• Place the empty pans on the opposite chairs, and put one compressed-towel capsule in each.

---

[23] For more on this concept, see Athanasius, *On the Incarnation of the Word*, especially pages 36-38.

When you're ready to start:

• Divide your students into teams of about 10.

• Line each team up behind the masking-tape line beside one of the chairs with a bowl of water (see diagram below).

• Give the first person in each team a plastic bathroom cup.

• Hold up one of the compressed-towel capsules and ask students, "Is this a towel?"

• Regardless of whether they answer yes or no, say, "This can be a towel, and you're going to make it one!"

• Tell them that when you say, "Go!" the first person is to dip a cupful of water, run to the other end, and pour it on his compressed towel. Then he runs back to the line and hands off the cup to the next person who does the same thing.

• The first team to grow its towel wins.

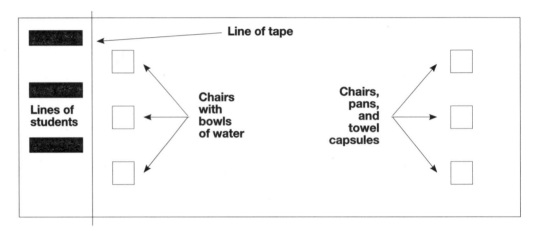

INTRODUCTION: MUSIC VIDEO

Play the music video, "The Scientist" by Coldplay (*A Rush of Blood to the Head*, 2002). You can stream it for free on http://music.aol.com if you have a laptop with Internet access. The full-screen resolution isn't the greatest, but it works. Make sure you watch the video beforehand in case there's questionable ad material before it. When you're ready, just hit play and make it full screen.

• *What is the singer trying to get across with this video?*

• *Why is it filmed in reverse?*

• *Can we go backward in real life?*

• *How does this video make you feel?*

Then say: *This is how the Israelites felt at this point in Ezekiel. They thought their hope was completely gone, and there was no throwing life into reverse to go "back to the start…"*

Have several volunteers read Ezekiel 37:1-14.

WHERE LIFE COMES FROM

• Ask: *How do you make puppies?*

• Say: *Now, it's clear you have to have dogs to mate with one another in order to have puppies. You can't just make them out of nothing. The same is true of us. You can't just make people out of nothing. And originally, all life was started by God.* Now this isn't a time to get bogged down in a lesson on evolution and creation. You'll have kids with differing views on this, so just get around it by saying: *God is the one who created and jump-started the earth. We're not going to get into specifics regarding how God created the world. The important thing to focus on is that all life comes from God. He started it, and God continues to keep it going.*

WHEN OUR LIVES ARE DEAD

Reread this sentence from verse 11: *"Our bones are dried up and our hope is gone; we are cut off."*

• *What sort of emotions do you suppose the Israelites must have been feeling when they said this?* Despair, hopelessness, sorrow—you name it. If the emotion is related to those three, they probably felt it.

• *Has there ever been a time in your life when you could relate to how the Israelites were feeling?*

• *Now, you don't have to tell specific stories about yourself or anyone else, but let's think of some categories that could lead people to feel the way Israel feels in this chapter.* This cry of Israel is one of hopelessness, of irrevocable (or so they think) circumstances. Many things in our lives create this sort of "there's no going back" feeling...Get your students to make a list of these.

• *What sorts of things make us lose hope?*

THE VALLEY OF DRY BONES

• *Now, this vision concerns a valley filled with dry bones. Does anyone here know anything about CPR? Okay, how do you rescue dry bones?* Obviously, you can't. Dry bones are the "deadest" you can get.

• *How many dry bones are there? Does this description ever mention anything about skeletons lying around?* This whole valley is full of dry bones, and never are they referred to as skeletons.

• *Describe what this might have looked like.* See, this wasn't a valley of wounded and dying people; this wasn't even a valley full of recently killed people. This is a valley full of scattered, dried-up bones (verse 2). A skull over here might go with the hip bone on the other side of the valley. Vultures and beasts of prey would have picked over these bones. There was no skin, no tendons, no muscles, no nothing. This isn't a case where you can shock a person's heart into beating again because it just stopped a couple of seconds ago—there were no hearts here! All that's left is bones—dry bones.

• Say: *This is what God uses as the symbol of what he will do to restore Israel.*

• *What happens to the bones?* The bones come together and line up where they're supposed to. Then the tendons and sinews grow back on, and the skin covers the bodies. But, there's no life in them. Then the LORD commands Ezekiel to prophesy to the breath—in Hebrew: *ruach,* the spirit—and command life to enter the dead people. Ezekiel does, and they live.

• *What is God trying to get across with this vision?* There's hope.

• Summarize: *God takes things that are disordered and scattered and dead, puts them back the way they're supposed to be, reattaches things, and then breathes life into them.*

• *We commented on the great number of bones, and in verse 11, God tells Ezekiel these bones represent the whole house of Israel. If we came across a valley of bones that had enough bones in it to represent everybody from an entire nation, what would we think had happened there?* Something horrible would have to have happened if there were that many bones in one place. "The sight suggests the remains of a major catastrophe."[24]

• Say: *And yet it's into these remains of a major catastrophe that God breathes his life-giving power and restores the life that was lost.*

YOU ALONE KNOW

• Say: *Another part of this passage worth noting is Ezekiel's response to God. In verse 3, the LORD asks him, "Son of man, can these bones live?" Now, up to this point in the Bible, there really isn't a tradition of people coming back from the dead. In 1 Kings 17:17-24, Elijah brings someone back from the dead, and in 2 Kings 4:18-37, someone comes back from the dead when his body touches Elisha's bones. But these people were recently dead. It's not as big of a stretch, per se, to think about them coming back from the dead. So on the surface, God's question seems preposterous. But then again, this is God.*

• *Ezekiel answers: "O Sovereign LORD, you alone know" (Ezekiel 37:3). What's significant about his response to God's question?* Ezekiel's reply leaves room for God to act.

• Explain: *Ezekiel recognizes God has control over life and death, and "he casts himself entirely upon the will and power of God."[25] This is the first thing we need to do to have God act in our lives. When we look at those things in our lives that seem dead, hopeless, and long gone, God would say, "Son or daughter, can your life live again?" And our response has to be, "You alone know."*

• *God tells Ezekiel to prophesy to the bones. God could have just raised them up; why do you suppose God told Ezekiel to prophesy to the bones? Did God need Ezekiel's help?* Just as Ezekiel could never have brought the bones back to life, we can't bring the things that are dead in our lives back to life, either. But just as God didn't resuscitate those bones without Ezekiel's participation, neither will he resuscitate our lives without our participation.

[24] Block, *The Book of Ezekiel: Chapters 25-48,* 374.
[25] Ibid., 375.

THE DESIRED RESULTS OF EXILE

Why are the people in exile again? They walked out of the covenant with God and thus walked away from his protection. *We've seen that God loves his people so much that he follows them into exile and goes to great lengths to try to win them back. Why does God do this?* Because God wants to be in relationship with them, and God doesn't want them to die. *See, only God can bring life to people, and it's only when we connect ourselves to God that we can receive that life we all need so desperately.*

Even when the Israelites are in exile, God hasn't left them, and he's working in that exile to bring about some specific results. The desired results of exile can be summarized in four "Rs": Return, Repentance, Resurrection, and Restoration.

• *Return: because there's no life outside of the relationship with God. When we're willing to return, that's the beginning of repentance.*
• *Repentance: because the covenant with God has been broken and acknowledgement of that fact is the key to resurrection.*
• *Resurrection: because God is into turning hopeless situations upside down and bringing life and restoration.*
• *Restoration: because God loves to bring people back into the life they were meant to live* (see session 11).

CLOSING

Pass out the journaling exercise, **Take Me Back to the Start**. Encourage your students to write to God about where they are. Play some meditative music during this exercise.

Station some of your leaders around the room, and let students know that if they want prayer for the restoration of something in their lives, they can go to one of the leaders and talk to them. Keep the music on, and station the leaders far enough apart—and far enough away from where the students are journaling—so that the students have privacy. Keeping the music on will prevent others from overhearing what the students have to say.

Have your worship band come back and play a praise song about God's healing, such as "There Is a Redeemer" by Keith Green (*Songs for the Shepherd*, 1986). If students are still praying with leaders, then sing several times, or go into another song from your worship set.

JOURNALING: TAKE ME BACK TO THE START

How did the music video make you feel?

How often have you felt like this in your own life? Can you remember the most recent time?

What is it that is dead or beyond hope in your life?

What do you need God to turn around?

Talk to God about what you're thinking and feeling right now…

RESTORATION TIME
SESSION 11: EZEKIEL 39:21-29; PSALM 139:13-16

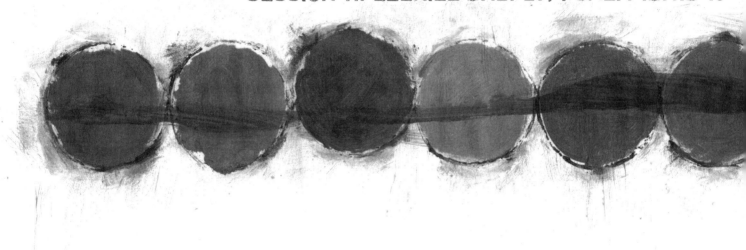

OVERVIEW

In line with this idea that you can run from God and mess your life up, it's reassuring to know God can not only resurrect and reconstruct the pieces of your life (see session 10), but also bring you back onto the path and the plan God's laid out for you.

SET UP

GAME

• Balloons

• Masking tape

• Pieces of cardboard (at least one foot by one foot; the shape doesn't matter, just the size)

• Thumbtacks

• Chairs arranged into a line

• Space in your youth room (see diagram for The Final Step game in the Making It Live for Your Students section)

ILLUSTRATION

• One ordinary calculator

MOVIE

• *Hitch*

SECTION 1: BACKGROUND FOR LEADERS

This section in Ezekiel is an excellent summary of the entire book. Israel was unfaithful to God, rebelled against him, and walked away from God; as a result, God hid his face (Ezekiel 39:23). Then, as a result of God hiding his face from Israel, their enemies conquered them, and they fell by the sword. God, as a holy and righteous God, has to respond to Israel "according to their uncleanness and their offenses" (verse 24). But as we've seen, that's not where God's intentions for Israel stop, and that's not where the story ends. As we saw in session 10, God can resurrect the scattered and broken pieces of our lives and breathe new life into them. We'll get an idea of what that new life looks like in session 12, but here in this session, we see the promised results of restoration.

FOR MY HOLY NAME

Here again in Ezekiel 39, we see more discussion of God acting for the sake of his holy name. For this discussion, here's another helpful perspective to consider: "Ezekiel will eventually claim that God will one day forgive, renew and restore, not because of anything anyone deserves, but solely because it is God's nature to do so."[26] So when God says in this chapter that he will be zealous for his holy name (verse 25), God's name represents his character and nature, not just his reputation. And it's in God's character to forgive and renew and restore. He delights in such things, as the parables of the lost sheep, the lost coin, and the lost son in Luke 15:3-32 clearly show. Our God loves finding people who are lost. He rejoices when they come running back home to him.

This God we see in Ezekiel, even though seeming strange at times and completely unlike what we're used to thinking about him, reveals he's the same God here as in the New Testament. All of this, from the visions of Ezekiel to the incarnation, are

[26] Gowan, *Theology of the Prophetic Books*, 128.

just steps of God's same plan to reveal himself to people so they can turn to him and live. Jesus coming to earth wasn't anything new in God's plan. He'd been planning it for all time and getting ready for it throughout the entire Old Testament period. This is one of the ideas that Ezekiel shows us here in this book.

The result of Israel's punishment is God's glory displayed among the nations (Ezekiel 39:21). And this display is interactive, because God uses the nations to attack Israel after her disobedience. So the nations attack Israel and carry off numerous people into captivity so the Israelites are scattered all over the world.

God's restoration, then, is interactive, in that he reaches in and brings his people out from among the nations, creating a powerful witness to the world that God is who he says he is and that he is all-powerful above all other gods. God is continually trying to get peoples' attention so they can turn to him and live. The entire book of Ezekiel is basically one multipart illustration of this truth.

BACK ON TRACK

Verses 25-27 tell us that only after God has brought Israel[27] out of captivity will the people know that he is the LORD. The knowledge that God is God comes after he restores them to the land. Then they have a chance to repent and realize what they've done wrong. This may seem backward, in that they're delivered from the consequences of sin before they've actually repented for it.[28] But it's important to keep in mind that we can't come to God on our own; God would be unknowable if he didn't come to us. Because God desires a relationship with us, he makes it so we can find him if we're looking; God's always right there waiting for us to turn and live (see also 18:23). It's God's initiative that allows us to respond and repent. So we can't even take credit for having made the effort to get that far to God. Every action on our part is a response to God who extends the gift—makes the opportunity; what's left for us is to receive it. This reminds me of what Paul says of our salvation in Ephesians 2:8-9: "For it is by grace you have been saved, through faith—and this not from yourselves, it is the gift of God—not by works, so that no one can boast." Our salvation is by grace, which is accepted by faith, which we wouldn't have if God hadn't given us the capacity to respond to him with the faith he placed in the heart of every person. So there we have it. It's really not us, and there's no credit we can take for our own salvation. It's God's initiative at every corner that makes it possible for us to live a new life in a relationship with him.

---

[27] Note: Jacob=Israel; if you'll recall when Jacob wrestled with God (see Genesis 32:22-31), God changed his name to Israel, and all 12 tribes are descended from his sons.

[28] Gowan, *Theology of the Prophetic Books*, 136.

SECTION 2: MAKING IT LIVE FOR YOUR STUDENTS

INTRODUCTION: THE FINAL STEP

• Before your group meets, blow up enough balloons for half the people you're going to use in the fourth step below.

• Have one piece of cardboard for every balloon you're going to use, and pin the balloons by their necks to the pieces of cardboard.

• With masking tape, make two lines on the floor as far apart in your room as possible. In front of one of the lines, create a line of chairs about three feet away so it forms a barrier. (See illustration.)

• Divide your group in half, or if you have a large group, select 10 to 12 volunteers and then divide them in half.

• Have one group stand behind each of the two lines you created.

• Give thumbtacks to the group behind the line that has the chairs in front of it.

• Give the second group the balloons attached to the cardboard. Take this group aside and tell them they're not to move or speak unless instructed by the person across the room from them. If the person they're paired with instructs them to come across the room, then they can come up to the line of chairs. You should have an equal number of pairs.

• Tell the group holding the thumbtacks that their job is to pop the balloon. They can do whatever they want, but they can only take one step. NOTE: You may also want to prohibit them from throwing the thumbtacks.

• Tell them to think carefully before they do anything.

• The first person to ask his or her partner to come across wins.

Leader Tip: The object is they have to ask their partners to come across to them, and then they only have to take one step to pop the balloon. This ties into our session, because that's what God does for us—only God doesn't even wait for us to ask him; God just comes across the gap that separates us and then leaves it up to us to take the last step. (NOTE: Don't say this yet…we'll discuss it later.)

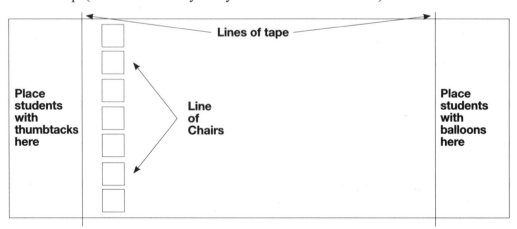

WHAT GOD IS DOING

Read Ezekiel 39:21-29.

Explain: *This passage is sort of a summary of the entire book because it gets at every-thing God has done or will do—including the judgment and why that came about, as well as what he intends to do for Israel in the future and what that will look like.*

MOVIE CLIP: *HITCH*—90 PERCENT OF THE WAY

Play the clip.
START [00:52:54] STOP [00:57:00]

• *Why is Alex so convinced that the perfect kiss is a 90 percent/10 percent deal?* This allows the woman to respond. That way the man isn't forcing himself on her.

• Say: *This is a good illustration of God's initiative toward us, except God comes 100 percent of the way, and then waits for us to decide if we want him. But what the movie clip illustrates so well is that forcing yourself on someone in a relationship is never a good idea. God will never force himself on us. He's there offering us all he has, but we still have to come to God.*

• *In the game we played, what was the key to winning?* The people holding the tacks had to ask their partners to come across the room.

• *After the people had come across the room, what was left for the people holding the tacks to do?* They only had to take one step.

Say: *In verses 21-24, God makes it very clear that he's using the exile as a punishment for Israel's unfaithfulness. But the punishment isn't his overall goal.*

• *What is God's overall goal in verses 21-24?* He wants the nations to see his glory.

• *Remember, you can't separate God's glory from God's self, so basically when you see God's glory, it's like seeing God. So then, what is the point of the nations seeing God?* God is doing all these things to put both his people and the nations of the world in a place where they can see who he is, so they have the option to come into relation-ship with him.

• Say: *Of course, not everyone will come into relationship with God, but they all will have the chance to see who God is. God has done everything to bridge the distance be-tween himself and us, but we have to walk "the bridge" to God.*

ALL MY DAYS

Pass around a Bible with Psalm 139:16 marked in it. Say: *This verse tells us God has a plan for us that includes all our days written out in his book before we'd even been born. Clearly, we can walk away from that plan, but God can bring us back, resurrect that which is dead, and restore us to the plan and path he has for us.*

Ask: *If, as we talked about with the movie* Hitch, *God will never force himself on us, what does that tell us we need to do to be part of his plan?* Sign up for it. Ask God to be involved in our lives. Take that last step of decision that God left up to us.

Conclude: *That one step of decision is all that's waiting between us and restoration, between us and allowing God's purposes to be worked out in our lives so we can be connected to the source of life and learn how to live again. God's desire for us is to know life with him—life beyond what we could have imagined or hoped for. That doesn't mean everything will suddenly be easy, but it does mean that no matter what happens, God is walking along with us and is working in everything for our good* (Romans 8:28).

ILLUSTRATION: ALL MY DAYS

Take your calculator out and ask a student how old she is. Type in that numeral and multiply it by 365 to get how old she is in days. (You can do this with several students if you have time.) Now, assuming she lives to be 90, she will live 32,850 days. If your average student is 15, she has more than 27,000 days left to live. And God has each one of them planned out! This gives new meaning to the idea that we need to turn our lives over to God day by day. Not only is God interested in the final outcome, he's interested in every single day of our lives as well…Now there's something to chew on.

CLOSING

Pass out the journaling exercise, **Signing Up for God's Plans**. Encourage your students to write to God about where they are. Put on some meditative music while they write.

JOURNALING: SIGNING UP FOR GOD'S PLANS

Read Psalm 139:13-16.

What does it mean for you to know that God personally knit you together while you were still inside your mother?

What do you think of the idea that you are fearfully (that means "awesomely") and wonderfully made?

What difference will it make in your life knowing that God has every one of your days already written down?

What difference will that make tomorrow?

Talk to God about how you feel about the fact that he cares about every day of your life...

SWIMMING LESSONS WITH GOD
SESSION 12: EZEKIEL 47:1-12; JOHN 7:38, 10:10

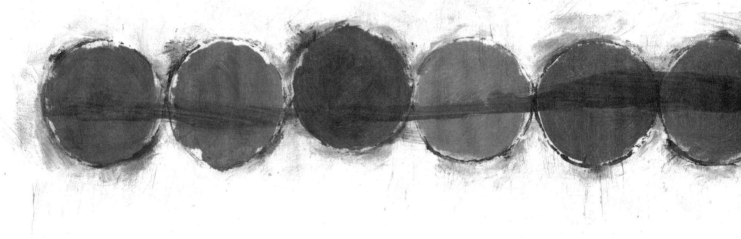

OVERVIEW

The river described in Ezekiel 47 behaves unlike any river we have ever experienced: It defies normal multiplication, geographic boundaries, crossing, and even death. If we thought we knew what water was, what it was for, and how to "swim" in it, then here's a swimming lesson that will blow your mind. If you go swimming in God's river, the possibilities are not only miraculous but also endless.

SET UP

ILLUSTRATION

- Two glasses, each half filled with water
- Several tablespoons of salt (in a separate container)
- A spoon

MOVIE

• *The Lord of the Rings - The Two Towers*

SONG

• "Dive," Steven Curtis Chapman (*Speechless*, 1999)

SECTION 1: BACKGROUND FOR LEADERS

THE KIND OF LIFE WE CAN JUMP INTO

We've come all the way to the end of the book of Ezekiel now, and we have a clear picture of just what God wants to do. He wants to give life. And this life defies description in that it's unlike anything we've ever seen before. The picture we're looking at for this session is indeed one that has to do with the end of time—with the new earth and a new city—a completely restored land. But the kingdom of God is here now, and we can take part in things that defy the "normal" way of doing things. The river we see in chapter 47 heals the land.

WATER THAT DEFIES "NORMAL" MULTIPLICATION

The first description of this water is in verse 2. The word used here implies a trickle, like water flowing out of a bottle. This is important, because as we follow Ezekiel as he wades out into the river, that trickle soon becomes a mighty flood.

The messenger wades downstream with Ezekiel in tow, and the water grows unlike anything that occurs in nature. Rivers don't grow unless they have other creeks or rivers flowing into them to provide more water. This water in verse 2 is only one trickle, and it becomes a river no one can cross (verse 5). The key is that this trickle flows from the temple of God (verse 1), and when the trickle comes from the temple, it doesn't need help to grow. The same is true of things God starts in our lives and in our ministries. They may seem to only trickle, but if they belong to God, they'll grow far beyond our natural abilities to make them increase or do well.

After measuring the exponential increase by walking off cubits, the messenger stops because the river is now at a point where it can't be crossed. Where the messenger stops is at the 4,000-cubit mark. Now, 1,000 cubits is about 1,700 feet, or about a third of a mile, which means in a mile and a third, the river has grown from a trickle that's less than what comes from your kitchen sink's faucet to a river that no one can cross. The messenger stops here, leaving both Ezekiel and us to imagine the river's exponential growth.

WATER THAT DEFIES CROSSING

Verse 5 tells us this river quickly became "a river that no one could cross." This is the second thing to notice about the life of God. Not only does the river's growth happen incredibly fast and without any normal sources of growth (nothing flowing into it), but the river also soon becomes uncrossable. When God starts moving his life and healing into people's lives, nothing can stand against his purpose. When God acts, no one can reverse what God brings about (Isaiah 43:13).

WATER THAT DEFIES TOPOGRAPHICAL BOUNDARIES

Then in Ezekiel 47:8, we see yet another so-called impossibility come to be. Daniel Block, in his commentary on Ezekiel, points out that "in order for the water to flow from Jerusalem to the Jordan Valley, it must flow down into the Kidron, up over the Mount of Olives, and then cross a series of valleys and mountain ranges before it reaches its destination."[29] The temple is in Jerusalem, and the place called "Arabah" in the NIV is the Jordan Valley. The Sea, of course, is the Dead Sea. The cool thing about this path is that the last time I checked, rivers only run downhill. I've never seen a river run uphill, much less cross several mountain ranges. This river defies topographical boundaries. But God doesn't see boundaries like we see boundaries. Boundaries or obstacles are nothing to this river, nor do obstacles stand a chance when God begins to move on our behalf in our lives. Ultimately, God's purposes will work out. Of course, that doesn't mean things will always go the way we think they should go, because God's ways are not our ways (Isaiah 55:8-9). But as we look back at what God's doing, we can see how his life is coursing through our lives and our world and bringing life where there was none, healing where there was pain, joy where there was only sorrow.

WATER THAT DEFIES DEATH

And finally, the river defies death. This river is a river of life. Ezekiel 47:8-10 tells us that it not only makes the salt water fresh, but it also provides for an abundance of living creatures.

Now, this concept of making salt water fresh is another impossibility. And this salt water is not just any salt water. The sea mentioned in these verses is the Dead Sea— 1,300 feet below sea level and 26 to 35 percent salt. At its low elevation, water flows into it but can't go anywhere except to evaporate. So all the salt stays in the water and has continued to become more and more concentrated over the years. In fact, the Dead Sea is so salty you can't drown in it—you float. It's actually possible to put your body completely upright in it, and you won't sink; you just sort of bob around like a loose cork. No amount of fresh water would get rid of all that salt. And yet, when this river touches it, it becomes fresh, and fish and other creatures can live in it again. That's why it's called the Dead Sea; nothing can live in it because it's so salty. But this river changes that. Everything the river touches lives. Everywhere the river

29 Block, *The Book of Ezekiel: Chapters 25-48*, 694.

goes, there's life. The life of God can touch things that people said were hopelessly dead, and God can cause them to live again—and they'll not only live but also produce life from such impossible things, such as the Dead Sea, or fruit like the trees that line the banks of this river (verse 12).

SECTION 2: MAKING IT LIVE FOR YOUR STUDENTS

MOVIE CLIP: *THE LORD OF THE RINGS - THE TWO TOWERS*

Unless you're sure all your students have seen the *Lord of the Rings* trilogy, prepare them for the clip by telling them the scene they're about to watch is almost at the end of the movie, which is the second in the series. This takes place in Isengard, which was where the evil wizard Saruman was making weapons in his tower to arm the orc armies of the dark lord Sauron. In the first film, *The Fellowship of the Ring*, we saw Isengard stripped so Saruman could do these terrible things. They pulled down the trees and turned what was once a pretty piece of the forest into a nasty hole for doing their dirty deeds. Now, in the last part of the second movie, we have this scene.

Play the clip. START [02:40:13] STOP [02:42:37] (All of chapter 49, "The Flooding of Isengard." Cues refer to the normal edition. In the extended edition, watch all of chapter 59.)

• Ask: *What did you like about this scene?*

• *How did it make you feel?* Hopefully, you have enough students who liked the movie, and you should get some positive responses about the water washing everything clean. If not, you may have to prompt them or share your own opinion. I know I was relieved both in the books and in the movies to get to this scene. You could almost smell the stench of the orcs—and to see all their greasy, slimy blackness and evil get washed away when the ents flooded Isengard was such a good feeling.

• Say: *This is only a glimmer of the sort of life and cleansing God is bringing to the land in the river we find in Ezekiel 47.*

WHAT THE RIVER DOES

Read Ezekiel 47:1-12 with your students.

• *Ask: What are some things about this river that jump out to you?*

• *What is the purpose of the river?* It's a river that brings life and healing wherever it flows.

• *We've talked about how God wants to restore Israel and work in our lives to restore things we thought could never be restored. What do you think the river could represent in this context of restoration?* The river represents life, and specifically, the life of God as it flows out of the temple and spreads out all over the place.

• *There are some interesting things we need to notice about this river we just read about…*

• *How do rivers get bigger?* They need streams and springs to flow into them to make them bigger.

• Explain: *The distance described in this chapter is about a mile and a third. In that short distance, the river Ezekiel is describing goes from a trickle—less than would come out of a faucet in your house—to a river that no one can cross. That's some serious growth without any streams or anything flowing into it.*

• *What direction do rivers flow?* Always downhill.

• *The next weird thing we need to notice about this river is that in order for it to follow the path we see in verse 8, the river would have to go through several valleys and mountain ranges in order to get to the sea. That means it had to go uphill!*

ILLUSTRATION: SALT IS SALTY

• Take the two glasses of water.

• Fill each half full.

• Pour salt into one of the glasses.

• Have a volunteer come and taste the water.

• Then, pour the fresh water from the other glass into the first glass.

• Stir.

• Have him or her taste the water.

• Ask: *Is the water still salty?*

• Explain: *The sea into which the river flows is the Dead Sea. Who can tell me something about the Dead Sea?*

• *The Dead Sea is called the Dead Sea because nothing can live in it—it's too salty. It contains more salt than any other body of water, and it's 1,300 feet below sea level. The Jordan River flows into it, but since it doesn't have an outlet, the water evaporates, leaving the salt. This has been happening for as long as you can imagine—and that results in a lot of salt.*

• *Now in our Ezekiel passage, the river described makes the salt water fresh. That's a miracle! It brings life into this sea where nothing can live. That's the life of God in action…*

RELATIONSHIP WITH GOD IS THE PREREQUISITE FOR LIFE

Say: *We see here that only in relationship with God can we really live. We can't walk away from the source of all life and expect to live. It's like unplugging the life support. We can't live without God. Way back in the garden, we were meant to live forever because of our relationship with God. Walking away from God took us out from under his protection and spurned his grace, and so the reality of death entered the picture. God has been pursuing us ever since, trying to get us to reconnect with our source of life—him—so we won't have to face eternal death. This is the story of the Bible. This is the story of the incarnation. Jesus said, "I have come that they may have life, and have it to the full"* (John 10:10). *This river in Ezekiel is definitely a picture of abundant life, and that's what Jesus came to let us experience.*

• *So the river is there. The life of God is there. How do we take part in this?* We have got to wade into the river just like Ezekiel did.

• *Imagine jumping into this river. What would happen?* Jumping into a river no one can cross means you'll get carried away.

• Summarize: *This is about surrendering ourselves to God and letting him work his will and plans in our lives. When we do this, streams of living water will flow from within us* (John 7:38). *If that's not taking part in the river, then I don't know what is.*

• *If we jump in, that water will get all through us—the life of God will saturate us—and then we'll start spilling over onto other people. Imagine that. A bunch of living fountains walking around spilling out living water wherever they go. Sounds like a miraculous growth to me.*

CLOSING: TAKING THE PLUNGE

Conclude: *So then, the decision is ours. The river is there. The life of God is real. It's up to us to decide whether we're going to jump. Take the plunge. Go for it without holding back. God wants to restore us, heal us, and give us his life. The question is, will you jump?*

Pass out the journaling exercise, **Taking the Plunge**. Encourage your students to write to God about where they are. Play "Dive" by Steven Curtis Chapman (*Speechless*, 1999; you can get the song from iTunes for $0.99) while they write.

JOURNALING: TAKING THE PLUNGE

Reread the description of the water's multiplication in Ezekiel 47:1-6.

What do you think?

What would jumping into the river and seeing what God has to offer look like in your life?

How do you feel about that?

What do you want to do? Will you jump?

Talk to God about what you're thinking and feeling right now...

BIBLIOGRAPHY

Allen, Leslie C. *Word Biblical Commentary, Vol. 28, Ezekiel 1-19.* Dallas: Word Books, 1994.

Allen, Leslie C. *Word Biblical Commentary, Vol. 29, Ezekiel 20-48.* Dallas: Word Books, 1990.

Athanasius. *On the Incarnation of the Word,* in *The Nicene and Post-Nicene Fathers.* Vol. 4 (second series). Grand Rapids: Eerdmans Publishing Company, 1956.

Aven, Anna. "Broken Promises." *Nelson's Annual Sourcebook for Youth Ministers.* 2005 Ed. Thomas Nelson Publishers, 2004.

Block, Daniel I. *The Book of Ezekiel: Chapters 1-24.* The New International Commentary on the Old Testament. Grand Rapids: Eerdmans Publishing Company, 1997.

Block, Daniel I. *The Book of Ezekiel: Chapters 25-48.* The New International Commentary on the Old Testament. Grand Rapids: Eerdmans Publishing Co., 1998.

Brueggemann, Walter. *An Introduction to the Old Testament: The Canon and Christian Imagination.* Louisville: Westminster John Knox Press, 2003.

Brueggemann, Walter. *The Land: Place as Gift, Promise, and Challenge in Biblical Faith.* Minneapolis: Fortress Press, 2002.

Gowan, Donald E. *Theology of the Prophetic Books: The Death and Resurrection of Israel.* Louisville: Westminster John Knox Press, 1998.

Lewis, C. S. *The Chronicles of Narnia.* One Vol. Ed. New York: HarperCollins, 2004.

The New Interpreter's Study Bible. New Revised Standard Version with the Apocrypha. Nashville: Abingdon Press, 2003.

Newsome Jr., James D. *The Hebrew Prophets.* Atlanta: John Knox Press, 1984.

Stott, John. *Romans.* Downers Grove: InterVarsity Press, 1994.

Stuart, Douglas. *Old Testament Exegesis.* 3rd Ed. Louisville: Westminster John Knox Press, 2001.

Thompson, Francis. "The Hound of Heaven." Abridged. www2.bc.edu/~anderso/sr/ft.html (accessed December 17, 2005).

Vawter, Bruce, and Leslie J. Hoppe. *Ezekiel: A New Heart.* International Theological Commentary. Grand Rapids: Eerdmans Publishing Company, 1991.

Webster's II New Riverside University Dictionary. Boston: New Riverside Publishing Co., 1988.

"Solomon's Temple." Wikipedia. http://en.wikipedia.org/wiki/Image:Solomon%27sTemple.PNG (accessed November 18, 2006).

Zondervan. *NIV Study Bible.* Fully Revised. Grand Rapids: Zondervan, 2002.